His Mission

Other Books by the Gospel Coalition

Don't Call It a Comeback: The Old Faith for a New Day, edited by Kevin DeYoung

Entrusted with the Gospel: Pastoral Expositions of 2 Timothy, edited by D. A. Carson

God's Love Compels Us: Taking the Gospel to the World, edited by D. A. Carson and Kathleen B. Nielson

The Gospel as Center: Renewing Our Faith and Reforming Our Ministry Practices, edited by D. A. Carson and Timothy Keller

Here Is Our God: God's Revelation of Himself in Scripture, edited by Kathleen B. Nielson and D. A. Carson

The Scriptures Testify about Me: Jesus and the Gospel in the Old Testament, edited by D. A. Carson

The Gospel Coalition Booklets Edited by D. A. Carson and Timothy Keller

Baptism and the Lord's Supper, by Thabiti M. Anyabwile and J. Ligon Duncan

Can We Know the Truth?, by Richard D. Phillips

Christ's Redemption, by Sandy Willson

The Church: God's New People, by Timothy Savage

Creation, by Andrew M. Davis

The Gospel and Scripture: How to Read the Bible, by Mike Bullmore

Gospel-Centered Ministry, by D. A. Carson and Timothy Keller

The Holy Spirit, by Kevin L. DeYoung

Justification, by Philip Graham Ryken

The Kingdom of God, by Stephen T. Um

The Plan, by Colin S. Smith

The Restoration of All Things, by Sam Storms

Sin and the Fall, by Reddit Andrews III

What Is the Gospel?, by Bryan Chapell

HIS MISSION

JESUS IN THE GOSPEL OF LUKE

D. A. CARSON AND
KATHLEEN B. NIELSON, EDITORS

WHEATON, ILLINOIS

His Mission: Jesus in the Gospel of Luke

Copyright © 2015 by The Gospel Coalition

Published by Crossway
    1300 Crescent Street
    Wheaton, Illinois 60187

Cover design: Dual Identity, inc.

First printing 2015

Printed in the United States of America

Trade paperback ISBN: 978-1-4335-4375-3
ePub ISBN: 978-1-4335-4378-4
PDF ISBN: 978-1-4335-4376-0
Mobipocket ISBN: 978-1-4335-4377-7

Library of Congress Cataloging-in-Publication Data

His mission : Jesus in the gospel of Luke / D.A. Carson and Kathleen B. Nielson, editors.
    pages cm
    "The Gospel Coalition."
    Includes bibliographical references and index.
    ISBN 978-1-4335-4375-3 (tp)
    1. Bible. Luke—Criticism, interpretation, etc. 2. Jesus Christ—Biblical teaching. I. Carson, D. A., editor.
BS2595.52.H57   2015
226.4'06—dc23   2014043717

Crossway is a publishing ministry of Good News Publishers.

VP		25	24	23	22	21	20	19	18	17	16	15
15	14	13	12	11	10	9	8	7	6	5	4	3	2	1

CONTENTS

PREFACE

The plenary sessions of the national conferences of The Gospel Coalition are always devoted to the exposition of Scripture. At the conference in April 2013, we focused on the Gospel according to Luke. A text that long and that rich cannot be given detailed treatment in eight expositions, but we decided that, instead of choosing a handful of contiguous chapters, we would in some degree cover the whole book. The slightly revised and printed manuscripts of those eight addresses constitute the eight chapters of this book. Each chapter stands alone, yet because we were all working on one biblical book, it is gratifying to see how well the individual chapters cohere and build on one another to provide a "feel" for this wonderful Gospel.

The appendix is a virtually verbatim report of a panel session that occupied another plenary hour. That panel was devoted to answering the question, "Did Jesus preach the gospel?" To those who are unaware of current debates, the question may seem a bit superfluous, almost insulting. Yet in recent years, very different answers have been given to that question. Some say, "No, Jesus didn't preach the gospel—he preached the kingdom, or the gospel of the kingdom." There may be a whisper of truth to this formulation, but it rapidly degenerates into a rather pathetic competition between the Synoptic Gospels and the letters of Paul. Others insist, "Jesus does *not* preach the gospel; he *is* the gospel." Once again, there is some truth in the formulation, for certainly Jesus did preach himself. But such a strong antithesis—he does *not* preach the gospel, he *is* the gospel—causes one to wonder exactly what the burden of Jesus's preaching ministry was, and why the first four books of the New Testament are called "Gospels." For others, the question is a trifle misleading: they argue that to grasp aright Jesus's significance, one not only must listen to what he preaches and teaches, but also observe what he does and what happens to him, including the cross and resurrection. Yet other answers are frequently advanced. So the question we posed became for our panel a trigger that prompted deeper reflection and better understanding of what we mean by the gospel of Jesus Christ. Besides, the panelists obviously enjoyed talking with one another, and their joy communicated itself to the audience, as it will communicate itself to readers.

I cannot adequately thank the plenary speakers for providing full manuscripts of their expositions. Thanks go to Daniel Ahn for the transcription of the panel discussion, to Kathleen Nielson for her thoughtful editing, and to Crossway for its commitment to this series. It is always a joy and a privilege to serve with people so transparently devoted to the Lord Jesus.

Soli Deo gloria.

Don Carson
President, TGC

1

JESUS THE SON OF GOD, THE SON OF MARY

Luke 1–2

John Piper

Only in one place in the Gospel of Luke does the author speak in the first person, referring to himself. He does this three times in the first four verses of the book:

> Inasmuch as many have undertaken to compile a narrative of the things that have been accomplished among *us*, just as those who from the beginning were eyewitnesses and ministers of the word have delivered them to *us*, it seemed good to *me* also, having followed all things closely for some time past, to write an orderly account for you, most excellent Theophilus, that you may have certainty concerning the things you have been taught. (Luke 1:1–4)

Never again does Luke refer to himself as "me" or "us" in this Gospel. And the reason he does it here is plain: he wants to come right out and be crystal clear about why he is writing this book. He is writing this account, he says, "that you [Theophilus, or John Piper, or add your name] may have certainty concerning the things you have been taught" (v. 4).

To Have Certainty

My focus in this chapter is on the first two chapters of the Gospel. We are not left wondering why Luke wrote these chapters. His purpose (that Theophilus will have certainty concerning the things he had been taught) is so explicit and so prominent at the beginning of the Gospel that I want to linger over it for a moment to clarify where this chapter is going.

Behind the translation "that you may have certainty" is the idea of knowing the "security," "safety," or "stability" of what you've been taught. The Greek word Luke uses, *asphaleian* (here translated as "certainty"), is used in two other places in the New Testament. One is Acts 5:23 (AT): "We found the prison locked in all security [*asphaleia*]"—usually translated "securely locked." The other is 1 Thessalonians 5:3: "While people are saying, 'There is peace and security [*asphaleian*],' then sudden destruction will come upon them." The same word is used nineteen times in the Septuagint (the ancient Greek translation of the Old Testament), where it almost always means "safety."

So the idea behind "that you may have certainty" in Luke 1:4 is that you may know not just the things you've been taught, but also something about them: their locked-down, secure, unshakable, solid, stable, immovable reality.

The Kind of Knowing That Lasts

I stress this not only because Luke puts it first, but because we live in a day when many Christians—perhaps like Theophilus—have been taught things, but they do not know those things this way. They know them the way one knows a cloud, not the way one knows a mountain. Viewpoints about God and the Bible, and right and wrong, float in people's minds, ready at any moment to be blown away by the slightest resistance and replaced by another cloud.

Luke does not want Theophilus—or you—to know these things that way. He wants us to know the *asphaleian* of the things—not just the things, not just the doctrines, but also the *asphaleian* of them. They are the kind of reality that is locked-down, secure, safe, stable, unchanging. I write my Gospel, says Luke, that you may know "the safety—the bolted-down security—the *asphaleian*" of what you've been taught. These things are safe from being stolen, safe from being changed, safe from ceasing to be what they are, safe from becoming unimportant or irrelevant, safe from not being reality anymore. These things, Theophilus, will always be. This is the kind of knowing that caused the church to survive through three centuries of frequent and terrible persecution. This is the kind of knowing that is immovable in the face of disease, abandonment, disillusionment, grief, and martyrdom. Luke has tended Paul's body through countless beatings and imprisonments (2 Cor. 11:23). He knows what kind of knowing lasts and what kind doesn't.

Most Excellent Danger

Luke knows the kind of knowing that tempts *"most excellent Theophilus"* (1:3). He writes about *"most excellent* Felix" in Acts 24. He writes about *"most excellent* Festus" in Acts 26. Luke tells us that most excellent Felix had "a rather accurate knowledge of the Way" (Acts 24:22), but he was alarmed at Paul's preaching, sent him away (v. 25), and then hoped for a bribe from him (v. 26). This is the kind of "accurate knowing" that destroys churches, leaves courageous Christians in jail, and brings the whole Christian movement into disrepute.

When Paul preached to "most excellent Festus," the governor said with a loud voice, "Paul, you are out of your mind; your great learning is driving you out of your mind" (Acts 26:24). And Paul said, "I am not out of my mind, most excellent Festus, but I am speaking true and rational words" (v. 25). It is dangerous to be a "most excellent" anything. Locked-down, secure, unchangeable knowledge has a way of troubling the rich and powerful. You can't buy truth with your riches. You can't control it with your power.

It's just too risky to know things that way. It doesn't give you enough wiggle room.

But this is what Luke is after for "most excellent Theophilus." He is saying: I am writing not just that you may know the things you've been taught about Jesus, but that you may know the *asphaleian* of them—the locked-down, unshakable, unchanging, absolutely secure reality of them. That you may know they *are*—like mountains, not clouds.

Weaving Together Jesus and the Baptist

How does Luke help Theophilus (and us) in Luke 1–2 know the securely locked-down, unchangeable nature of the reality of what he's been taught? He does it by weaving together the stories of Jesus and John the Baptist—the announcements of their births, the ways they were conceived, the ways they were born, the songs their parents sang over them, and even an encounter between them while they were still in the wombs of their mothers.

And in telling these stories of John and Jesus, Luke makes clear and solid the most important realities in the universe: God, Christ, salvation, and faith. That's my outline. First, Theophilus, I want you to know the *asphaleian* of God.

1. The Certainty of God

"Zechariah was serving as priest before *God*" (Luke 1:8). Gabriel appeared to him and said, "I stand in the presence of *God*" (v. 19). Zechariah's son, Gabriel said, "will turn many . . . to the Lord their *God*" (v. 16). Later, "Gabriel was sent from *God*" to the Virgin Mary (v. 26) and said: "You have found favor with *God*" (v. 30); "The Lord *God* will give [your son] the throne of his father David" (v. 32); "The child . . . will be . . . the Son of *God*" (v. 35); and "Nothing will be impossible with *God*" (v. 37). Then Mary sang, "My spirit rejoices in *God*" (v. 47). When John was born and Zechariah's mouth was opened, he worshiped, saying, "Blessed be the Lord *God*" (v. 68). When Jesus was born, "a multitude of the heavenly host [praised] *God*" (2:13), saying, "Glory to *God* in the high-est" (v. 14). When Jesus was presented in the temple, Simeon took him up "and blessed *God*" (v. 28). Old Anna gave "thanks to *God*" (v. 38). And Jesus as a boy "increased in wisdom and in stature and in favor with *God* and man" (v. 52).

In case Theophilus misses the point about God, Luke makes the same point about the Lord. Zechariah and Elizabeth walked "blame-lessly in all the commandments and statutes of the *Lord*" (1:6). There appeared to Zechariah "an angel of the *Lord*" (v. 11), who told him his son would be "great before the *Lord*"(v. 15). The angel said he would "make ready for the *Lord* a people prepared" (v. 17). When Elizabeth conceived, she said, "Thus the *Lord* has done for me" (v. 25). The angel came to Mary and said, "The *Lord* is with you!" (v. 28). She responded, "I am the servant of the *Lord*" (v. 38). When Elizabeth met Mary, she said, "Blessed is she who believed that there would be a fulfillment of what was spoken to her from the *Lord*" (v. 45). Then Mary sang over her son, "My soul magnifies the *Lord*" (v. 46). All the friends of Elizabeth heard "that the *Lord* had shown great mercy to her" (v. 58). When her son, John, was born, "the hand of the *Lord* was with him" (v. 66). His father prophesied over him, "You, child, will be called the prophet of the Most High; for you will go before the *Lord*" (v. 76). When Jesus was born, "an angel of the *Lord*" came to the shepherds (2:9). They spoke of "this thing . . . which the *Lord* has made known to us" (v. 15). And in the temple, Mary and Joseph presented Jesus "to the *Lord*" (v. 22), ac-cording to what was written "in the Law of the *Lord*" (v. 24).

WHERE "GOD CENTERED" COMES FROM

Sometimes people wonder where phrases such as "God saturated," "God besotted," and "God centered" come from. They come from Bible stories like this. This story is mainly about God. God is the main actor in this story. He is central, dominant, and all-pervasive. And if you stretch your view out over the whole Gospel, it's still true. Matthew uses the words *God* and *Lord* 59 times, but Luke

194 times—three times as often—even though the two Gospels are almost identical in length. Luke also uses the terms three times as often as Mark and about twice as often as John.

Most excellent Theophilus, here is the first locked-down, unshakable, secure, mountainlike reality in everything you've been taught: *God is real. God is active. God is unstoppable.* God sent his angel. God struck Zechariah dumb. God made the barren Elizabeth and the Virgin Mary conceive. With God, nothing is impossible (1:37).

And when we get to the end of the story, Luke tells us that Jesus was "delivered up according to the definite plan and foreknowledge of *God*" (Acts 2:23), and that "Herod and Pontius Pilate, along with the Gentiles and the peoples of Israel, [were gathered] to do whatever [God's] hand and [God's] plan had predestined to take place" (4:27–28).

Theophilus, mark this one down. *God is the main reality in the universe. God is the main reality in history. God is the main reality in this Gospel. He is all-planning, all-pervasive, all-powerful.* Know the *asphaleian* of the doctrine of God—the locked-down, unshakable, never-changing, ever-relevant, mountainlike reality of God.

2. The Certainty of Jesus

Second, Theophilus, know the secure, solid, unshakable reality of Jesus:

> "And behold, you will conceive in your womb and bear a son, and you shall call his name Jesus. He will be great and will be called the Son of the Most High. And the Lord God will give to him the throne of his father David, and he will reign over the house of Jacob forever, and of his kingdom there will be no end."
>
> And Mary said to the angel, "How will this be, since I am a virgin?"
>
> And the angel answered her, "The Holy Spirit will come upon you, and the power of the Most High will overshadow

you; therefore the child to be born will be called holy—the Son of God." (Luke 1:31–35)

The first clue for Theophilus that something really extraordinary is happening in history is the word of Gabriel that Jesus will reign over the house of Jacob forever and his kingdom will have no end (v. 33). A king is about to be born, Gabriel says, whose kingdom will never be overthrown. It will outlast every other kingdom, and therefore it is a universal kingdom, not just a Jewish kingdom, though it clearly fulfills all the Old Testament Jewish hopes. This king will reign over the house of David.

But God could raise an ordinary man from the dead and make him an eternal messiah-king. So God did something at this birth to make clear that Jesus was no ordinary man. God himself, by the Holy Spirit, brought into being a man who was infinitely more than a man. The "therefore" in the middle of verse 35 links the work of the Holy Spirit in this conception with the title *Son of God*: "The Holy Spirit will come upon you, and the power of the Most High will overshadow you; *therefore* the child to be born will be called holy—the Son of God."

AN UTTERLY UNIQUE SONSHIP

This is not sonship like the sonship all believers have with God. We are born according to the flesh and then reborn by the Holy Spirit. Jesus was not born by the union of a man and a woman, but by the supernatural work of the Holy Spirit replacing the seed of a man. Born of Mary, Jesus was fully human; the Holy Spirit so united the eternal second person of the Godhead with Jesus's human nature that Jesus was and is simultaneously truly human and truly God, with a human nature and a divine nature united in one person.

There are two more pointers to this in the context. When pregnant Mary went to visit pregnant Elizabeth, John the Baptist leaped in his mother's womb, and Elizabeth was filled with the Holy Spirit, crying out a blessing that included these words: "And why is this granted to me that the mother of my *Lord* should come to me?"

(Luke 1:43). The word *Lord* is used twenty-eight times in Luke 1–2. All of them refer to God. Even here Elizabeth was speaking by the Holy Spirit, and in the same breath said, "Blessed is she who believed that there would be a fulfillment of what was spoken to her from the *Lord*" (Luke 1:45). So she used the word *Lord* for the God who spoke through Gabriel *and* for the child in Mary's womb.

THE LORD'S CHRIST AND CHRIST THE LORD

Similarly, we get the double use of the title *Lord* in relation to the title *Christ*. Luke says that it had been revealed to Simeon "that he would not see death before he had seen the *Lord's* Christ" (Luke 2:26). And the angels said, "Unto you is born this day in the city of David a Savior, who is Christ the *Lord*" (Luke 2:11). This Jesus is the Lord's Christ, and he is Christ the Lord.

So, Theophilus, the second reality that is locked-down solid, safe, and sure like a mountain range of glory is that a king has been born who fulfills all the dreams of Israel, who will reign forever until every kingdom is his kingdom, and who is the one and only Son of God by virtue of his two natures, one fully divine from eternity past and the other fully human as he was made flesh. This Jesus, Theophilus, is the Lord. This Jesus is God.

3. The Certainty of Salvation

Third, Theophilus, know the unshakable, locked-down, never-to-be-altered reality that this Jesus saves his people from their sins by dying in their place.

At his birth, the angels said, "For unto you is born this day in the city of David a Savior" (Luke 2:11). Zechariah said, God "has raised up a horn of salvation for us" (1:69). And how would this salvation come? From what do we most need saving? Zechariah, filled with the Holy Spirit (v. 67), said of his son John, "You will go before the Lord to prepare his ways, to give knowledge of salvation to his people in the forgiveness of their sins" (vv. 76–77).

Theophilus, you are a sinner. You need a Savior who can deal with your sins and forgive them. This Jesus, this God-man, is your Savior. He dealt with your sins and forgave them. How did he do that? He set his face to die for you. He said, "The Son of Man must suffer many things and be rejected by the elders and chief priests and scribes, and be killed, and on the third day be raised" (Luke 9:22). This was his plan, his mission.

NEW-COVENANT BLOOD

Why? How could this save anyone? It saves because his blood is the blood of the new covenant in which God promised to forgive the sins of his people: "I will make a new covenant. . . . I will forgive their iniquity, and I will remember their sin no more" (Jer. 31:31, 34). And at his Last Supper, Jesus took the cup and said, "This cup that is poured out for you is the new covenant in my blood" (Luke 22:20).

That is how sins are forgiven. That is how he is a Savior. That is how Zechariah's prophecy was ultimately fulfilled (1:76–77). In the old covenant, animal sacrifices were offered over and over again. In the new covenant, Jesus "suffered once for sins, the righteous for the unrighteous, that he might bring us to God" (1 Pet. 3:18).

So, Theophilus, know the *asphaleian*—the locked-down, absolutely secure, never-changing reality of your God, of the God-man Jesus Christ, and of your salvation in the forgiveness of your sins by the shedding of his blood. Know these things like you know mountains, not like you know clouds.

4. The Certainty of Faith

Fourth, Theophilus, know with rock-solid, unshakable certainty that there is a way for you to have this salvation and a way for you to miss it. I speak to you now as to *"most excellent* Theophilus." I have shown you the work of God in history; now be sure you see the work of God in the soul. God has brought salvation into history. Now God brings the human soul into salvation.

God's salvation has happened in real, locked-down, totally

fixed, secure, non-mythological, unchangeable history. This history is populated with real people: Herod, king of Judah; Zechariah, priest of the division of Abijah; Elizabeth, of the daughters of Aaron; Caesar Augustus, the Roman emperor; Quirinius, governor of Syria; Jesus, born in Bethlehem, blessed in Jerusalem, and raised in Nazareth, not Olympus. This is dateable history, not fiction. Know the solidity and reality of this, Theophilus.

RESPONDING LIKE MARY

And just as real, unalterable, and historical as the way salvation came into history is the way the human soul enters into salvation. It is possible to miss salvation, Theophilus. Just because Jesus came into the world does not mean that you will come into him.

Don't miss this, Theophilus—don't miss the difference between Zechariah's response to the good news and Mary's response. Gabriel was sent from God (Luke 1:26). He brought an old and barren couple (Zechariah and Elizabeth) spectacular news: they would have a son, and he would be the long-expected, Elijahlike forerunner of the Messiah (1:17). But Zechariah did not rejoice at this. He questioned, "How shall I know this?" (v. 18). Theophilus, this is not the way to receive the news of salvation.

The angel answered him with indignation: "I am Gabriel. I stand in the presence of God, and I was sent to speak to you and to bring you this good news. And behold, you will be silent and unable to speak until the day that these things take place, because you did not believe my words, which will be fulfilled in their time" (Luke 1:19–20). When God sends his word of salvation to you, Theophilus, this is not the way to enter it.

Look, rather, to Mary, to whom God also sent the angel Gabriel, who said:

> Do not be afraid, Mary, for you have found favor with God.
> And behold, you will conceive in your womb and bear a son,
> and you shall call his name Jesus. He will be great and will be
> called the Son of the Most High. And the Lord God will give

to him the throne of his father David, and he will reign over the house of Jacob forever, and of his kingdom there will be no end. (Luke 1:30–33)

And Mary did not say, "How shall I know this?" God had told her it would be. She said, "How will this be, since I am a virgin?" (1:34). The angel answered her question and told her how it would be. The Holy Spirit would do this thing (v. 35). And the angel gave her more hope: *nothing will be impossible with God, and your barren relative Elizabeth is six months pregnant.* To this, Mary responded, "Behold, I am the servant of the Lord; let it be to me according to your word" (v. 38).

MARY'S SONG OF FAITH

What do you call this response, Theophilus? I'll tell you what you call it. You call it what Elizabeth called it. When she and Mary met, Elizabeth said, "Blessed is she who *believed* that there would be a fulfillment of what was spoken to her from the Lord" (1:45). Zechariah did not believe the word of God (v. 19). Mary did.

Then she sang. She sang for you, *most excellent* Theophilus. She sang a song of faith for you:

My soul magnifies the Lord,
    and my spirit rejoices in God my Savior,
for he has looked on the humble estate of his servant. . . .
And his mercy is for those who fear him
    from generation to generation.
He has shown strength with his arm;
    he has scattered the proud in the thoughts of their hearts;
he has brought down the mighty from their thrones
    and exalted those of humble estate;
he has filled the hungry with good things,
    and the rich he has sent away empty. (Luke 1:46–53)

Be humbled, most excellent Theophilus, be brought low before the might and the mercy of the God of Israel. Let no office, no power, no wealth, and no pleasure make the faith of Mary too hard for you. There is one way into this salvation. It is not the way of wealth, the way of power, or the way of doubt. It is the way of faith. God has acted. God is speaking. Trust him. If you would go down to your house justified, join the lowly and say, "God, be merciful to me, a sinner!" (Luke 18:13).

How to Have This Salvation

Beware, most excellent Theophilus, of banking on your wealth: "It is easier for a camel to go through the eye of a needle than for a rich person to enter the kingdom of God" (Luke 18:25). But you *can* enter. Mary has made that plain: "What is impossible with man is possible with God" (18:27; 1:37).

Do not boast in your uprightness, Theophilus. Rather, when you have done all that you were commanded, say, "We are unworthy servants" (Luke 17:10). But don't despair. Though you are not a Jew, Simeon has made it clear: *Jesus is for everyone*, "a light for revelation to the Gentiles, and for glory to [God's] people Israel" (2:32). There is hope for you—and all Gentiles—most excellent Theophilus, but you must humble yourself: "Whoever does not receive the kingdom of God like a child shall not enter it" (18:17).

Salvation has come into the world, Theophilus. Know the rock-solid, objective, unalterable factuality of the unfathomable, mountainlike truths of God, of the God-man Jesus Christ, and of salvation in the forgiveness of sins by his new-covenant blood.

But also know this: there is a way to enter this salvation, and there is a way to miss it. "Enter through the narrow door. For many, I tell you, will seek to enter and will not be able" (Luke 13:24). Renounce all reliance on your wealth, your power, your office, and your uprightness, and receive this salvation like a child, like Mary.

Ringing with Joy

And one more thing, Theophilus. Have you noticed? This story rings with joy. The angel to Zechariah: "You will have *joy* and *glad-*

ness, and many will *rejoice* at [John's] birth" (Luke 1:14). John himself could not even wait to be born before he rejoiced in Jesus; as Elizabeth said to Mary, "When the sound of your greeting came to my ears, the baby in my womb leaped for *joy*" (v. 44). So Mary sang her *Magnificat*: "My soul magnifies the Lord, and my spirit *rejoices* in God my Savior" (vv. 46–47). When John was born, all the neighbors *rejoiced* with Elizabeth (v. 58). And when Jesus was born, the angelic announcement came, "Behold, I bring you good news of great *joy*" (2:10).

Theophilus, you have now heard of the Holy Spirit. By him was the God-man, Jesus Christ, conceived in a virgin's womb. All this joy is his work. This is his great work. John, filled with the Holy Spirit (Luke 1:15). Zechariah, filled with the Spirit (v. 67). Elizabeth, filled with the Spirit (v. 41). Simeon, covered with the Spirit (2:25).

The Happiest Story in the World

Do you have the Holy Spirit, Theophilus? The great mark of the followers of Jesus is the joy of the Holy Spirit. And the great mark of that joy is that it magnifies the Lord: "My soul magnifies the Lord, and my spirit rejoices in God my Savior" (Luke 1:46–47).

Know this, Theophilus. I have written these things, most excellent Theophilus, that you may know this *asphaleian*, this certainty. It is a locked-down, rock-solid, unshakable, unalterable reality. God is the great actor and the great goal of this story. He is at the beginning, planning all things; he is in the middle, governing all things; and he is at the end, being magnified in all things. Jesus Christ, the God-man, is his divine Son. Salvation is his glorious work. And childlike faith is your way in. Go join the shepherds, Theophilus, glorifying and praising God (Luke 2:20). Be filled with the Holy Spirit. This is the happiest story in the world.

2

JESUS DESPISED

Luke 4:14–30

Colin Smith

Grace is a double-edged sword. It attracts and it repels. To some, it brings the savor of life; to others, it has the smell of death. Preachers of grace are loved and despised.

That's how it was with Jesus from the beginning of his public ministry, which Luke introduces with the account of our Lord's visit to his hometown of Nazareth (Luke 4:14–30):

> And he came to Nazareth, where he had been brought up. And as was his custom, he went to the synagogue on the Sabbath day, and he stood up to read. (4:16)

This event took place about a year into the ministry of Jesus. If we had only Luke's Gospel, we might assume that Jesus launched his ministry from home soil, but this was not the case. Matthew and Mark both record the return to Nazareth later in the ministry of Jesus (Matt. 13:53–58; Mark 6:1–6), and John tells us about the early days of Jesus's ministry in Cana, Capernaum, and Jerusalem (John 2:1, 12, 13).

Consistent with the other Gospels, Luke tells us that news about Jesus had already spread throughout the surrounding country

(Luke 4:14). Jesus had been ministering in Galilee, and reports of his miracles in Capernaum had made their way back to Nazareth before Jesus returned to his hometown (v. 23).

It is easy to imagine the interest, curiosity, and conversation all the reports of Jesus's great works would have aroused in Nazareth. Children who had grown up with Jesus and had played with him in the streets were now in their thirties, many of them married with their own children. Some of the folks in this small town would have owned tables or chairs that Jesus had made or mended in the carpenter's shop. And, since it was our Lord's custom to worship in the synagogue, we can safely assume that some in the congregation at Nazareth had sat or knelt beside him in worship without ever guessing the identity of their fellow worshiper.

But now everyone was talking about Jesus, and when someone from a small town becomes famous, it's a big deal for everybody else. That would have been the case especially in Nazareth, which wasn't exactly on the top ten list of desirable places to raise a family! The longsuffering townsfolk there had to live with the miserable saying, "Can anything good come out of Nazareth?" (John 1:46). Well, now it seemed that they might have an answer to that: "Everyone's talking about Jesus! Well, guess where he comes from? He was raised in Nazareth!"

Finally, the great day came. After all the words that had been spoken and all the stories that had been circulated, Jesus was back in Nazareth, "where he had been brought up" (Luke 4:16). Word would have gone around quickly. Everyone knew they had better get to the synagogue early. There was sure to be a really big crowd.

A Service Unlike Any Other

You don't need me to tell you how dreary so much that passes in the name of religion can be. How dull, how oppressive and tedious, how deadly boring it can all become: instruction from an ancient book, the dead weight of endless traditions, the pious superiority of some clerical gentleman.

But on this day, it was different.

The synagogue service would have followed a familiar pattern: the singing of psalms, the recitation of the *Shema*, a pronouncement of blessings, followed by a reading from the Law of Moses and then another from one of the prophets. It was at this moment that Jesus stood up:

> The scroll of the prophet Isaiah was given to him. He unrolled the scroll and found the place where it was written,
>
> "The Spirit of the Lord is upon me,
>   because he has anointed me
>   to proclaim good news to the poor.
> He has sent me to proclaim liberty to the captives
>   and recovering of sight to the blind,
>   to set at liberty those who are oppressed,
> to proclaim the year of the Lord's favor." (Luke 4:17–19)

Jesus chose the reading, which was from Isaiah 61, and announced these great promises of Scripture with the ownership and authority of the One who had come to fulfill them. Then "he rolled up the scroll and gave it back to the attendant and sat down" (v. 20), which, of course, was what all rabbis did when they were about to teach.

The tension and anticipation in the room must have been electric as everyone waited for Jesus to speak:

> And the eyes of all in the synagogue were fixed on him. And he began to say to them, "Today this Scripture has been fulfilled in your hearing." (vv. 20–21)

We are given only the opening line of Jesus's sermon here, but what a line it was, and what a sermon it must have been! It was unlike anything those in the synagogue that day had ever heard.

The Preaching Ministry of Jesus

What we have here is a fascinating insight into the preaching ministry of Jesus. Our Lord's proclamation bears four distinguishing marks that set the trajectory of preaching for all of us who share the privilege of speaking in his name today.

1. Jesus Applied the Scriptures to the Lives of His Hearers

Notice first that Jesus preached the Scriptures. He read from the book of Isaiah, then spoke about it. This was not unusual. The congregation in the synagogue would have been well used to a scribe, Pharisee, or layperson talking about Moses, Isaiah, or one of the other prophets.

People in many churches are familiar with this too. A learned person gets up and begins to speak in a monotone voice:

"Please turn in your Bibles to the prophet Isaiah . . ."

People settle down as the preacher gets into his stride:

"Isaiah ministered during the reigns of Uzziah, Ahaz, Jotham, and Hezekiah . . ."

A few folks take quick looks at their watches: How long will this be going on?

"Here, in these words, the prophet speaks about a day to come, when the Lord will visit his people . . ."

So much preaching can seem like a lecture about prophecies from the past or promises for the future, leaving ordinary people in the pew asking, "What in the world does this have to do with me today?"

But look what happens when the Bible is in the hands of Jesus! Prophecies from the past and promises for the future become gifts for today through Jesus Christ. *Today, this Scripture has been fulfilled in your hearing!* There was no wistful nostalgia for some golden age in the past, no sentimental platitudes about hope for a better world in the future. No! Christ said, "I am here to tell you there is hope for you today!"

No wonder the eyes of all in the synagogue were fixed on him. He was speaking to them! He was speaking for today! And what he spoke was good news.

What we see in the preaching ministry of Jesus is surely a pattern for all of us who have the privilege of speaking in his name.

Christ took the Word that was "there and then" and brought it into the "here and now." The message was not that God had done great things for others, but that the God who had done great things for others was ready to do great things for Jesus's hearers—and that he would do them through Jesus himself.

J. I. Packer says that "the proper aim of preaching is to mediate meetings with God."[1] Christian preaching is more than imparting information from the Bible. It is God's means of bringing transformation through his Word. The test of our preaching is not whether our people can pass an exam in Bible knowledge, but whether they have encountered God and experienced the life-changing effects of his Word in their lives. This is what happened when God's Son opened God's Word.

Preaching that mediates encounters with God comes through preachers who encounter God for themselves. They know that the first step in preparing to speak from the Bible is to let the Bible speak to them. So they open the Bible, submitting their lives to its searching power, and come before God in the spirit of Frances Ridley Havergal's prayer:

Lord speak to me, that I may speak
In living echoes of Thy tone.[2]

The greatest demand on all who are called to preach is that we put ourselves through the mangle of God's Word as it searches and sifts our hearts every week. And our greatest blessing is that by

[1] *Truth and Power* (Downers Grove, IL: InterVarsity Press, 1996), 120.
[2] From the hymn "Lord, Speak to Me, That I May Speak" by Frances R. Havergal, 1872.

this Word, God brings strength, comfort, peace, and hope—first to us and then, through us, to others.

2. Jesus Spoke Directly to the Human Condition

Jesus identified four kinds of people to whom he brings good news: the poor, the captives, the blind, and the oppressed (Luke 4:18). The Bible uses these words to describe the condition not of some people, but of *all* people before God.

To those who are wealthy, Jesus says, "What does it profit a man to gain the whole world and forfeit his soul?" (Mark 8:36). To folks who make much of their freedom, he says, "Everyone who practices sin is a slave to sin" (John 8:34). To people who feel that they can find their own way to God, Scripture says, "the God of this world has blinded the minds of the unbelievers" (2 Cor. 4:4).

So when Jesus announced good news for the poor, the captives, the blind, and the oppressed, he was not saying that he came into the world for particular groups of disadvantaged people. He was describing the spiritual condition of all people. Norval Geldenhuys writes:

> It is a characteristic of the Savior's preaching, that he referred in a remarkably plain manner to the unfathomable spiritual need of mankind. . . . Sin makes a man inwardly poor . . . makes him a captive to its stranglehold, makes him spiritually blind, so that he loses all vision and all power of clear judgment, and crushes his personality.[3]

The clarity of our Lord's description of the human condition is a powerful model for all of us who speak in his name today. Christian preachers are not called to flatter the already overinflated egos of lost people. Our commission is to speak the hope of the gospel with clarity and with compassion into the dreadful reality of our fallen human condition.

---

[3] *The Gospel of Luke* (London: Marshall, Morgan & Scott, 1977), 169–170.

3. Jesus Preached Himself

It is striking that Jesus's message was focused on himself:

> The Spirit of the Lord is upon *me*,
>> because he has anointed *me*
>> to proclaim good news to the poor.
> He has sent *me* . . ." (Luke 4:18)

Christ preached himself, and those who speak in his name must proclaim him also. Luke records that when Jesus spoke, "the eyes of all in the synagogue were fixed on him" (v. 20). Good preaching always fixes the eyes of those who hear on Jesus.

Some years ago, I was given a sabbatical and had the opportunity to hear many sermons preached in churches from widely different traditions. I was struck by how often a supposedly "Christian" sermon began and ended without any explicit reference to Christ our Savior. Christ preached himself, and we must do the same. What good will your sermon do, what hope or comfort can it bring, if Christ is not it?

4. Jesus Proclaimed Grace

Grace was clearly the central theme of Christ's ministry at Nazareth. As the people heard him speak, this was what impressed them most, and their first response was to marvel at *"the gracious words that were coming from his mouth"* (Luke 4:22).

Our Lord's communication of grace would have been evident to the congregation in Nazareth from his announcement that he had come *to proclaim the year of the Lord's favor* (v. 19). The Lord's favor was an outpouring of grace, and the year of the Lord's favor was the pinnacle of some wonderfully compassionate laws that God gave to his people Israel.

One of these laws was that every seven years all debts were to be cancelled (Deut. 15:1–2). Imagine if that was the law in America today. Suppose the people at Visa and MasterCard decided that every seven years they would wipe the whole slate clean and allow all their customers to start again with zero balances!

But in God's laws for Israel, that was only the beginning. At the end of every seven years, when debts were cancelled, slaves were also to be released (Deut. 15:12–14). When folks in ancient Israel were unable to pay their debts, they could fulfill their responsibilities to their creditors by offering their labor in the place of the money that they could not pay. But God said that this kind of arrangement could not continue beyond the seventh year.

Then God gave his most radically compassionate law of all. In the fiftieth year, after seven cycles of seven years in which releases of debts and servants were given, the trumpet was to be sounded and a jubilee proclaimed in the land. In the time of Moses, when God was sustaining his people in the wilderness, he gave a command regarding the property that would be entrusted to them:

> You shall consecrate the fiftieth year, and proclaim liberty throughout the land to all its inhabitants. It shall be a jubilee for you, when each of you shall return to his property and each of you shall return to his clan. (Lev. 25:10)

When God's people entered Canaan, God gave a portion of land to each tribe and to each family, and the jubilee law was given to make sure that it stayed that way. Over the years, some people would find it necessary to sell their land, but once in every lifetime, in the fiftieth year, land that had been bought was to be returned to the family of original ownership.

This meant that land was held on a kind of leasehold basis, in which its price or value was determined by where the nation was in the fifty-year cycle. A year before the jubilee, the price of land would be low, because the buyer could hold it for only one year before the trumpet would sound for its return to the original owners. But for those purchasing land a year *after* the jubilee, the price would be high, because the land could be held for forty-nine years, bringing the profit of multiple harvests before the trumpet would sound for the land to be returned.

These were marvelously compassionate laws. They placed a check on the growing power of those who accumulated wealth, making sure that their children would have to find their own way rather than simply floating through life on their massive inheritances. At the same time, these laws gave a new start to the poor and oppressed once in every lifetime. No other nation has ever had laws like these. No culture has ever protected the poor like this.

How would you have liked to live under these laws? Your answer will depend largely on whether you would have been a borrower or a lender. These laws were great for debtors, but they were very costly for creditors. But God had said, "You are my people, and this is what you are to do when I bring you into the land I will give you."

How often do you think this year of jubilee happened? Never! Not even once![4] It is not difficult to work out why. The folks with the power were the folks with the money, and when they looked at what the jubilee would cost them, they decided against it. So the trumpet never sounded; the year of the Lord's favor was never proclaimed. And this flagrant flouting of God's laws continued for centuries. No wonder the Old Testament prophets were so scathing about the oppression of the poor when God's laws for their protection were so consistently ignored.

Surely it is not surprising that Israel turned a blind eye and a deaf ear to these costly commandments. God's compassionate laws could operate only through people who loved God with all their hearts and loved their neighbors as much as they loved themselves. And that has never been the case in any country or culture. God's law shows us how selfish we really are.

So God spoke through Isaiah about the One who would come and do what had never been done before: proclaim the year of the Lord's favor. The Spirit of the Lord would be on him, anoint-

---

[4] "There is no historical record, biblical or extrabiblical, that Israel ever once observed the Jubilee year." Kevin Howard and Marvin Rosenthal, *The Feasts of the Lord* (Nashville, TN: Thomas Nelson, 1997), 197.

ing him to proclaim good news to the poor and freedom for those who were oppressed. It was a marvelous promise, but who would have the authority to do this, and who would be willing to pay the price?

No one in the entire history of Israel had ever come close to fulfilling this promise—until Jesus came to the synagogue at Nazareth, took the scroll from the attendant, unrolled it to the place where Isaiah prophesied the jubilee, and said, "The Spirit of the Lord is upon me, because he has anointed me . . . to proclaim the year of the Lord's favor." Then, with the eyes of everyone in the synagogue fixed on him, he said, "Today this Scripture has been fulfilled in your hearing."

"God is going to do for you," Jesus was saying, "what you would not do for each other. He is going to cancel all your debts to him. He is going to set you free from Satan's power and give you back the inheritance that Adam your forefather lost." That's the promise of the gospel, and it is marvelous news.

But the year of the Lord's favor, which brings such joy and blessing to us, came at incredible cost to Jesus. Think about this: if you write off a debt of a thousand dollars, you are down by a thousand dollars yourself. When God writes off our debt to him, he absorbs the loss in himself, and this is why Jesus went to the cross. He bore the loss to cancel our debt and to restore our lost inheritance. God cancelling debts in Christ! God releasing captives in Christ! God restoring lost inheritances in Christ! That's the gospel.

The Winsome Power of Preaching and Personifying Grace

It is hardly surprising, then, that "all spoke well of him and marveled at the *gracious words* that were coming from his mouth" (Luke 4:22). Grace was what struck them when they listened to Jesus, and they marveled because it was not what they were used to hearing.

Exhortations to duty and morality would have been the staple diet for these folks in the synagogue at Nazareth, as they are the staple diet for millions of people today. Travel the world and listen to what is being said in sermons preached in mosques, in synagogues, and even in many churches, and you will find that the message is about what you *must* do for God or what you *should* be! But listening to Jesus, the people of Nazareth knew that they were hearing something completely different. They hadn't heard anything quite like it before. *Gracious words* were coming from his mouth, and the people were amazed.

If you have been shaped by a form of religion that is more associated with harshness than with grace, you are not alone. I have a dear friend who served the Lord faithfully as a pastor at great personal cost. He endured many trials, the greatest of which was the early death of his wife from cancer. At one point in his grief, I discovered that he had stopped attending the church where he lived. It was out of character for him, so I asked him why. "Colin," he said, "it was like being hit over the back of the head with a two by four every Sunday, and I just couldn't take it any longer."

This was not what the people of Nazareth experienced while listening to Jesus. "The law was given through Moses; grace and truth came through Jesus Christ" (John 1:17). The glory of Jesus is that he is *full of grace and truth* (v. 14). Grace was the message and grace filled the messenger.

There is a remarkable passage in the novel *Jane Eyre* by Charlotte Brontë. The character Jane often reflects Brontë's own experience, and at one point she describes going to church and hearing a gifted young preacher:

> The heart was thrilled and the mind was astonished by the power of the preacher, [but] neither was softened. Throughout there was a strange bitterness, an absence of consolatory gentleness. . . . And when he had done, instead of feeling better, calmer, more enlightened by his discourse, I experienced an inexpressible sadness. For it seemed to me . . . that the eloquence to which I had been listening had sprung from a heart where lay turbid depths of disappointment, where moved troubling impulses of insatiate yearnings and disquieting aspirations.

I was sure that the preacher, pure-minded, conscientious, zealous as he was, had not yet found the peace of God that passeth all understanding; he had no more found it, I thought, than I.[5]

I wonder how often Christian congregations have experienced that kind of sadness. Here was a man talking about peace while evidently not enjoying it himself. The man in the pulpit can talk about faith, humility, patience, and grace, but a strange sense of unreality hangs over the congregation if there is little evidence of these things in his life. From such emptiness, dear Lord, deliver us. Fill all who speak in your name so that the reality and power of your grace may be known.

The Double-Edged Sword of Grace

There is an extraordinary twist in this story. To our great surprise, the people who at first spoke well of Jesus and marveled at his gracious words subsequently "drove him out of town and brought him to the brow of the hill on which their town was built, so that they could throw him down the cliff" (Luke 4:29).

Why was there such an extraordinary change of attitude toward Jesus? Luke records that "when they heard these things, all in the synagogue were filled with wrath" (v. 28). What were "these things" that so quickly turned the benevolent and appreciative congregation at Nazareth into a mob bent not only on evicting Jesus from their town, but on destroying him altogether? The answer, in a word, was grace. Grace caused them to marvel and grace filled them with fury.

No Obligations

People get angry about grace because grace means that God has no obligations. We can never place him under our control. The people of Nazareth felt that they had a special claim on Jesus because, after

---

[5] Quoted in W. G. Blaikie, *For the Work of the Ministry* (London: Strahan and Co., 1873), 52.

all, it was his hometown. And surely it stood to reason that since he was doing miracles for others, he should give priority to performing a few for the people with whom he had grown up. After all, charity begins at home!

The people from Jesus's hometown felt that he had an obligation to them. Jesus knew what they were thinking, so he said to them: "Doubtless you will quote to me this proverb, 'Physician, heal yourself.' What we have heard you did at Capernaum, do here in your hometown as well" (Luke 4:23).

Christ does not do miracles on demand. Grace is given freely. You can't demand it. It cannot be earned or deserved. But here, it seems, was a group of people who felt that Jesus *owed them* some mighty works. Nazareth was his hometown, and they believed that they had a right to see his power on display.

But rights are always based on law. For example, you might have a right to a tax refund. If you do, it is because the paying of taxes is based on law and the law regulates the amount of taxes to be paid. Rights and law always come together. However, as soon as you come into the world of grace, you leave the world of law and rights behind. Grace means that something is given freely and without obligation. There are no rights in the world of grace.

This is where the people of Nazareth got into difficulties, as many still do today. The tragedy was that the people who felt Jesus owed them found that no mighty works were done in their town. People who think it is their right receive nothing from Christ. God does not bless on demand.

W. G. Blaikie points out that culture has inverted the message of the Christmas angels. They said, "Glory to God in the highest; on earth, peace, goodwill to men." Our culture says, "Glory to *man* in the highest; on earth, peace, goodwill to God!"[6] It's all about us, and we have assumed the role of telling God what he must do. We approach God with our list of demands and give him our commandments: "Thou shalt give us what our hearts desire. Thou

---

[6] *Glimpses of the Inner Life of Our Lord* (London: Hodder and Stoughton, 1876), 130.

shalt bless and affirm us in all that we do. Thou shalt keep thyself out of our public square and out of our private lives, and so long as *man* is in the highest place, we will observe peace and goodwill toward God!"

It might surprise you to know that Blaikie was specifically describing Scottish culture in the nineteenth century—which shows that nothing much has changed! What happened at Nazareth happens in every culture. Our default approach to God is to tell him what he must do for us. But grace means that God has no obligations, and that makes people angry.

No Restrictions

Grace also means that God has no restrictions. God is free to bestow his blessing wherever he chooses, and this is the main point of two stories to which Jesus referred as he addressed the people of Nazareth.

The first of these is the story of the widow of Zarephath (Luke 4:25–26). At a time of severe drought and famine, God sent the prophet Elijah to a widow in Sidon. Sidon was the heartland of idolatry and the homeland of Jezebel, the notoriously wicked queen. But grace means that God has no restrictions, so he was free to send Elijah, along with the blessing that came with him, to a widow in, of all places, Sidon!

Making the point painfully clear, Jesus said, "There were many widows in Israel in the days of Elijah . . . and Elijah was sent to none of them but only to Zarephath, in the land of Sidon, to a woman who was a widow" (v. 26). This woman experienced the miracle of God's provision. Her jar of flour did not run out and her jug of oil did not run dry.

God can bring his blessing wherever he chooses. Grace means that he has no obligations and no restrictions. No one has a right to grace and no one can be excluded from grace.

Then Jesus followed up by mentioning the story of Naaman, making the same point but with a fascinating contrast (v. 27).

Naaman was the captain of the Syrian army, so while the widow of Zarephath was desperately poor, Naaman was at the opposite end of the economic spectrum. Picture this man wearing the military decorations that reflect his distinguished career. But Naaman had a problem: he had contracted the dreaded disease leprosy. He knew that he was in trouble, so he came to Elisha the prophet, who told him to wash in the Jordan River. In a miracle of God's grace, Naaman was wonderfully healed.

Again driving the point home with wonderful clarity, Jesus said, "There were many lepers in Israel in the time of the prophet Elisha, and none of them was cleansed, but only Naaman the Syrian" (v. 27). Think of it! Naaman was the captain of the armies of the *enemies* of God's people, and God's blessing came to him! Grace means that God is obliged to save no one and that he is free to save anyone. God is not subject to demands or restrictions. Grace means that God has free will. Our God is in heaven and does whatever pleases him (Ps. 115:3).

The people of Nazareth could not lay claim to God's blessing any more than the widow of Zarephath could be excluded from it. The person who, like Naaman, seems furthest from God's blessing may receive it, while one who seems closest may go without it.

When the people of Nazareth heard these things, "all in the synagogue were filled with wrath" (Luke 4:28). Grace is a double-edged sword. It draws and it offends. It amazes and it infuriates. Grace will either make you angry or it will lead you to worship.

Does it not amaze you, brother or sister, that you should be a Christian when some whom you know and love see nothing great in Christ? Why is this? You won't want to claim that you are a better person or that you made better choices. Surely you will choose rather to stand before God with a sense of wonder and amazement at the unmerited operation of his grace in your life. In a way that you will never be able to fully explain or understand, God has laid hold of you and turned you around in Jesus Christ.

Kent Hughes tells a moving story about a large and prestigious church in England that had several mission halls in poor areas of the city under its care. The church's tradition was that on the first

Sunday of every year, the people who worshiped in the mission halls would gather with those in the prestigious church to share a Communion service.

On one of these occasions, the pastor of the church saw a man who had once been a burglar kneeling to receive Communion. The man had been wonderfully converted and had joined one of the mission halls. Remarkably, the man kneeling beside him at the Communion rail was the judge who, some years before, had sent this man to prison for his crimes. The pastor was deeply moved at how grace had touched the burglar's life and the wonderful change that had come to this man.

After the service, the pastor caught up with the judge and asked him, "Did you see who was kneeling beside you at the Communion rail this morning?"

"Yes," said the judge. "It's a miracle of grace." And then he said it again: "It is a miracle of grace."

"Yes," said the pastor, "it really is marvelous to think of how he has been converted from a life of crime."

"No," said the judge. "I wasn't talking about him. I was talking about me! It's no great surprise to me that the burglar came to Christ. He knew the extent of his need. But look at me. I was taught from infancy to live like a gentleman, that my word was my bond, that I should say my prayers and go to church. I went to Oxford, obtained my degrees, was called to the bar, and eventually became a judge. I was sure that I was all I needed to be, though I too was a sinner. Pastor, for me to see my need of Christ—*that* was a miracle of grace."[7]

We worship a God who reserves the right to swoop down uninvited into human lives and begin a work of grace. God's freedom to do this without obligation and without restriction gives us hope as we pray for lost people, whether they seem near or far from God. Grace means that God is free to move into any life at any time. He does this through the gospel. Let grace lead you to worship and fire you up for a life of gospel ministry.

---

[7] Kent Hughes, *Luke,* Preaching the Word Commentary Series, vol. 1 (Wheaton, IL: Crossway, 1998), 146.

3

JESUS'S TRANSFORMING POWER ON BEHALF OF THE AFFLICTED

Luke 8:26–56

Crawford Loritts

Have you ever felt beaten down and desperate? Perhaps that's where you are now—overwhelmed, out of options, and in need of God's intervention.

In 2002, in the space of about thirty-six hours, I received an avalanche of bad news. I had just returned home after visiting my sister, who had had surgery. The surgeon was cautiously optimistic that he and his team had removed all of the cancer cells. Then I got a call informing me that that was not the case. She had also contracted a virus and wasn't expected to survive. Then I got another call from our oldest son, who was rushing to the hospital with his infant son, our first grandchild, who had a very high fever and had suffered a seizure. Then the phone rang again. My wife's aunt, who was more like a second mother to her, had just died unexpectedly. On top of all of this, I was right in the middle of dealing with a crisis facing our ministry.

This rapid sequence of events sent me a very clear message:

Crawford, you can't handle this. This is the time for aggressive surrender and dependence. You need God to step into what you and Karen are facing. Get to God, and he will get to what you are facing. His presence is what you need.

This is what you feel, what you sense, as you read Luke 8:26–56. Jesus confronted amazing, devastating need and dramatically delivered each of the three people in this passage. At first glance, it is tempting to conclude that these are three isolated encounters— miracles—that stand on their own. But they are connected. As we will see, the demon-possessed man, the woman with the hemorrhage, and the ruler's daughter had some things in common.

I want to summarize these remarkable encounters, underscore what they have in common, and then identify three specific applications for us.

Encounters

First, Jesus encountered a demon-possessed man (Luke 8:26–39).

Jesus and his disciples came to the area around the small town of Gera, on the eastern shore of the Sea of Galilee. They ran into a man who was totally under the control of demons. He was naked and living, thankfully, in isolation among the dead, or "the tombs" (v. 27). He was in an awful, powerless condition.

To say that he was infested with demons is an understatement. In fact, when Jesus asked the man his name, he replied, "Legion," because "many demons had entered him" (v. 30). To gain some perspective on that name, we might recall that *legion* was a Latin term denoting about six thousand (that's right, six with three zeros!) Roman soldiers. Now, we don't know for sure if this man had that many demons in him, but the point is that he was tormented and totally controlled by an insurmountable host of evil, fallen angels. And Jesus confronted the demons.

Second, Jesus encountered a woman who had been bleeding nonstop for twelve years (8:43–48).

Jesus, along with his disciples, was actually on his way to heal the daughter of Jairus, a "ruler of the synagogue" (v. 41). However, at this point, the crowds were attracted to and enamored with Jesus. His fame, based on the stories of the miracles he had performed and the people he had helped, went before him and spread like wildfire. The people were drawn to him like flies to honey. It is not an overstatement to say that he was mobbed. According to the last line of verse 42, "As Jesus went, the people *pressed* around him." In that crowd was a woman who was out of options. She came in contact with Jesus and touched his clothes. And Jesus healed her.

Third, Jesus encountered Jairus's daughter (8:40–42, 49–56).

The press of the crowd and the healing of the woman delayed Jesus's arrival at Jairus's house. As a result, before he got there, Jairus's daughter died. When he finally arrived, he was met with weeping and mourning (v. 52). When Jesus said, "Do not weep, for she is not dead but sleeping," they laughed at him (vv. 52–53). It's as if they were saying: "Come on, now. You can't be serious! Look at her. She's dead, and you got here too late!" But Jesus raised her from the dead.

Commonalities

What do a demon-possessed man, a woman who had been bleeding for twelve years, and a dead girl have in common? Again, at first glance, you would think that these were isolated encounters meant to stand alone. But look closely. Luke grouped these encounters because, among other things, he wanted us to see clearly and to embrace what these people faced, felt, and experienced. These three who were healed had at least these three things in common.

First, they had no control over their afflictions and conditions.

The demon-possessed man was tormented and controlled by demons. Can you imagine the torture that he endured? I doubt very seriously that this man wanted to be considered weird and abnormal. He did not want to do what he did, but his alienation and bondage were out of his control. In fact, it appears that he had grown so accustomed to his bondage and demonic domination that he, and others for that matter, no longer distinguished between who he was and who he had become; he was simply "a man . . . who had demons." Perhaps he had embraced a sort of "comfortable demise," for he begged Jesus not to "torment" him (Luke 8:28). He was powerless to change what he had become, and he knew it.

The woman with the hemorrhage for twelve years was battered by her disease. It is important to note that there was nothing that she or anyone else could do about her condition. By this time, she knew that her affliction was not some temporary discomfort or passing embarrassment that would eventually go away. It had gone on for twelve years! Neither she nor the professionals could rein in or stop the bleeding. Look again at the description of the seemingly bleak finality of her situation and condition: "though she had spent all her living on physicians, she could not be healed by anyone" (Luke 8:43). What's more, according to Leviticus 15:25–30, the hemorrhaging made her ceremonially unclean—and therefore she was not allowed to participate in any social or worship gatherings. Anyone who touched her would also be declared unclean. This must have made her feel terribly alone and isolated. She was powerless, with no control over her miserable circumstances.

Then there was the synagogue ruler Jairus. His twelve-year-old daughter was sick and dying. The text doesn't identify the illness or disease that had a death grip on his little girl, but she was declining rapidly. Jairus's position, contacts, and resources could not turn things around. He and his wife could not do anything to stop what appeared to be the inevitable. Their little girl was slipping out of their hands. They were losing her, and they were powerless, with absolutely no control over her condition and what appeared to be an unimaginable, painful conclusion.

Second, it is obvious that all three were out of options on the human level.

I want to press into this because helplessness is the incubator for hope. In all three cases, there were no human solutions. Their ends were apparently irreversible and sure. Others had given up on them by either staying away from them (the demon-possessed man) or by sending the message in so many words, "The end is at hand, get your house in order" (the hemorrhaging woman and the dying girl).

But in the cases of both Jairus and the woman, their conditions and their powerlessness fueled desperation. Look at what Jairus did: "And falling at Jesus' feet, he implored him to come to his house, for he had an only daughter, about twelve years of age, and she was dying" (Luke 8:41–42). Then there was the woman, whose sickness had stripped her of everything she had and who bore the embarrassment and stigma of being ceremonially unclean. She could not enjoy close contact and fellowship with the people she knew and loved. But instead of shrinking back and giving in to the "inevitable," she was desperate to come in contact with Jesus. She pressed through that mob, where no doubt many hands were pulling at Jesus, and came in contact with his body. "She came up behind him and touched the fringe of his garment" (v. 44).

At the end of the line, filled with desperation, there was only one final option on the table—Jesus. I can imagine the thoughts racing through their minds: "I heard that he performed miracles. . . . Will he heal me? . . . He's my only hope. . . . I heard that he can set me free. . . . I've got to get to Jesus."

Third, when the demon-possessed man, the hemorrhaging woman, and Jairus's family came in contact with Jesus, they encountered God. In short order, they dramatically experienced and learned that there is no sickness, disease, or condition that is greater than Jesus and beyond his ability to handle.

These desperate people became objects of miraculous mercy and compassion. For example, when Jesus cast the demons out of the man, the people could not believe what they had seen. This wild, evil, violent, tormented, naked man was suddenly "sitting at the feet of Jesus, clothed and in his right mind" (Luke 8:35). But Jesus not only restored the man; in his love and compassion, he commissioned him to minister to others. Jesus directed him to "return to your home, and declare how much God has done for you" (v. 39).

And imagine what the woman must have experienced when she made her way through that crowd and, in one last desperate gesture, touched just the fringe of Jesus's garment. The text says that *"immediately* her discharge of blood ceased" (v. 44). But there was intense drama in this encounter. As soon as the woman touched just the fringe of his clothes, Jesus said, "Who was it that touched me?" (v. 45). Peter was confused, so he turned to Jesus and said, "Master, the crowds surround you and are pressing in on you!" (v. 45). In other words, "Jesus, virtually everybody is touching you." But what Jesus felt from that dear woman was the touch of desperation and faith. That's why he said to Peter in verse 46, "Someone touched me, for I perceive that power has gone out from me." Then, in love and compassion, Jesus restored her dignity and honored her faith. He tenderly called her "daughter" and said to her, "Your faith has made you well; go in peace" (v. 48). There was no shame, fear, or isolation. Jesus had made her whole.

But in the case of Jairus's little girl, it appeared that Jesus had, as the saying goes, missed the window. Jairus was with Jesus when the woman was healed, and while Jesus was speaking, someone from Jairus's household delivered the tragic news: "Your daughter is dead; do not trouble the Teacher any more" (Luke 8:49). What Jairus feared most had happened. But Jesus turned to Jairus and said, "Do not fear; only believe, and she will be well" (v. 50). Mind you, Jairus had just witnessed a miracle, and I believe Jesus's promise was validated by what Jairus had just seen.

When they finally arrived at Jairus's house, the professional mourners were there. Jesus told them to stop weeping because the little girl "is not dead but sleeping" (v. 53). But when Jesus said the girl was sleeping, he was not saying that she wasn't dead or implying that she was in a coma. He was saying that her death was not final. Jesus simply ignored the incredulous mourners, turned to the child, took her by the hand, and said two words: "Child, arise" (v. 54). And she did! Her parents were amazed.

These three encounters reveal and underscore the deity and lordship of Christ. Jesus is Lord over demons—ask the demon-possessed man. Jesus is Lord over disease—ask the woman who hemorrhaged for twelve years. Jesus is Lord over death—ask Jairus, his wife, and their twelve-year-old daughter.

Each of these encounters foreshadowed the victory of the cross. When Jesus cast out the demons, he was giving the Devil a preview of his coming defeat. Ultimately, sickness and disease are the result of sin. When Jesus healed the woman, this too pointed to the cross, where sin would be dealt a death blow. When Jesus raised Jairus's daughter from the dead, he was pointing to his own death and his resurrection. Death is defeated. This is the victory of the cross!

Keep in mind that these miracles happened to honor and glorify God. These dramatic displays of Jesus's glory give us a glimpse of who he is and what he can do. He doesn't always choose to work in these ways. Because we don't experience physical healing or see someone raised from the dead does not necessarily mean that our faith is weak or we don't have the right kind of faith. Keep in mind that 100 percent of the people whom Jesus healed eventually died, including Jairus's daughter. God does what he does for his glory. He will not be manipulated, and sometimes he says no.

Implications

Three compelling implications and lessons emerge from these three incredible, dramatic encounters with Jesus.

First, our faith grows in direct proportion to our desperation. Do we really want God to step into our challenges? Are we hungry for him? Is he our everything? Are we really convinced that we can't make it without him?

Second, inadequacy and suffering are our friends. They are holy handicaps that keep us tied to the heart of Jesus. The gaps and adversity we experience are God's reminder that every second we need him. We were born to depend upon God.

Third, Jesus wants to speak life into our dead circumstances.

He himself is life. There is no situation or circumstance that is beyond the life-giving, redemptive reach of our Savior. Where there is Jesus, there is hope.

Perhaps you have heard the story of the master chess player who saw in a store window a painting entitled "Check-mate." It depicted two chess players, one of whom, as the title suggests, had been put in check. Game over. As he studied the painting, something bothered the master chess player. Then it dawned on him. The artist had made a mistake. There was one more move.

Jesus is never out of options and he doesn't have to search for solutions. He is the solution to our dilemmas, pain, and afflictions. Run to him. Trust him.

4

JESUS'S RESOLVE TO HEAD TOWARD JERUSALEM

Luke 9:18–62

D. A. Carson

One of the things that we sometimes overlook when we study the Gospels is that each is ordered a little differently from the others. Part of the reason why we overlook this point springs from the way most of us have our devotions: chapter 3 today, chapter 4 tomorrow, chapter 5 the next day—and by the time we read chapter 4, we have forgotten chapter 3, and by the time we reach chapter 5, we have forgotten chapter 4, and so forth. As a result, our reading of Scripture sometimes becomes bitty.

But reading each Gospel straight through at a single sitting enables us to see the unique organization and order of each book, and therefore to learn some things in the Word of God that a more bitty reading may overlook. To take a very easy example, in Mark's Gospel, miracles are scattered here and there throughout the book, and each is thematically tied to its own context. Matthew picks up a lot of those same miracles, but he puts them all into chapters 8 and 9. So we have Matthew 5, 6, and 7—the Sermon on the Mount, a collection of great teaching—then chapters 8 and 9—a collection of spectacular miracles. The same authority of Jesus that stands behind the teaching also stands behind these powerful miracles, by which Jesus heals the sick, casts out demons, stills the storm, and so forth. Clearly Matthew decided to adopt, at various points, a topical organization. Chapter 10 breaks off in a new direction again.

There's nothing wrong with this (so long as an author is not pretending to be giving us a chronological order when he is giving us a topical order). The Holy Spirit, in giving us these Scriptures, has led these writers to do things differently so that we gain different slants and insights from the different Gospels.

About twenty-five years ago, I read the great biography of Oliver Cromwell by Antonia Fraser titled *Cromwell: Our Chief of Men*. Chapter by chapter, she follows his chronology until she gets to the years of the Protectorate, and then she writes four chapters that are purely topical in organization. Once they are behind her, she returns to a chronological ordering. Similarly, the Gospel writers were capable of structuring their books in diverse ways in order to enable us, their readers, to see things from slightly different angles.

The passage before us draws attention to an ordering that is unique to Luke. Luke 9:51:

> As the time approached for him to be taken up to heaven, Jesus resolutely set out for Jerusalem.[1]

When you read the other Gospels, you discover that Jesus goes back and forth between Galilee and Jerusalem several times. But here in Luke's Gospel, only at chapter 9, Jesus already is resolved to head toward Jerusalem in some final sense.

Some people have called this Luke's travel narrative because now, in his ordering of things, Luke emphasizes again and again that Jesus is going to Jerusalem to die and to rise again. As the chapters unfold, Luke keeps reminding us of this point:

Then Jesus went through the towns and villages, teaching as he made his way to Jerusalem. (13:22)

Now on his way to Jerusalem, Jesus traveled along the border between Samaria and Galilee. (17:11)

Jesus took the Twelve aside and told them, "We are going up to Jerusalem, and everything that is written by the prophets about the Son of Man will be fulfilled. He will be delivered over to the Gentiles. They will mock him, insult him and spit on him; they will flog him and kill him. On the third day he will rise again." (18:31–33)

After Jesus had said this, he went on ahead, going up to Jerusalem. (19:28)

In other words, everything that takes place in Luke's Gospel from 9:51 on takes place under the looming shadow of the impending cross. That is one of the ways Luke organized his material. That is the way God has given us this book.

Let us begin by considering Luke 9:18–56. And let us ask: How are the sections here linked? I propose to run quickly through the passage that is before us and show a couple of important lessons that we learn from reading this book in the light of the cross.

I want to make two important assertions that arise from reading the book of Luke humbly and carefully.

The Misunderstood Messiah

In his own time, Jesus is the misunderstood Messiah, but Luke's readers see what Jesus's contemporaries do not see—Jesus is resolved to go to Jerusalem to die and rise again. We shall see how that is worked out in five sections of this chapter.

Not a Conquering King

First, Jesus is God's Messiah, but this Messiah will suffer, die, and rise again (vv. 18–26).

You may be familiar with the event that takes place in Caesarea Philippi. Jesus asks his disciples, "Who do the crowds say I am?" Eventually, Peter gives a straightforward answer that Jesus approves: "God's Messiah." Luke preserves a briefer version of Peter's answer than the longer one preserved in Matthew 16:16: "You are the Messiah, the Son of the living God," that is, "You are the Christ" (*Messiah* and *Christ* mean the same thing). That means that Jesus is the fulfillment of Jewish expectations. *Messiah* simply means "someone who is anointed." In the Old Testament, kings and priests, and sometimes prophets, were anointed. That is why at least some Jews in Jesus's day anticipated the coming of two messiahs—a kingly messiah and a priestly messiah. In the Gospels, the term most commonly refers to the anticipated kingly messiah: to say that Jesus is God's Messiah means he is the promised King in David's line. He is the Anointed One; he is the King; he is the Christ.

But the fact is that when Peter makes that confession, he does not mean exactly what you and I mean when we make that confession. When you and I speak of Jesus as the Messiah, we cannot help but include in that confession the assumption that Jesus is the Messiah *who went to the cross, died, and rose again.* At this point in his pilgrimage, however, Peter doesn't have that category. That is made very clear in Matthew's and Mark's tellings of this incident, but it is hinted at in Luke, too. It shows up in Matthew and Mark because when Jesus goes on to talk about his impending death, Peter says: "Never, Lord! This shall never happen to you!" (Matt. 16:22)—which shows that at this juncture, he cannot conceive of a crucified messiah. Messiahs win, he thinks; messiahs rule; messiahs reign—especially a messiah like this one, with spectacular miraculous powers at his disposal. What Peter means by confessing that Jesus is the Messiah is not all that the Bible teaches about Jesus as the Messiah. What he says is the truth, and he is blessed by Jesus for speaking the truth. He has some genuine insight and conviction on the matter, but it is not full Christian truth.

A similar point surfaces in Luke 9:21. After Peter confesses that Jesus is the Messiah, Luke comments, "Jesus strictly warned them not to tell this to anyone." Why not? If he is the Messiah, why not announce it? There are different reasons for Jesus's reticence in different parts of the Gospels, but here the plain reason is what they mean by *messiah*. What the crowds understand by this word is so bound up with triumphalism, sovereignty, and reign *without the cross* that in some ways Peter's confession clutters up the expectations. Jesus is more likely to acknowledge who he is without cavil when he is talking to people in the pagan, heathen side of Galilee than when he is talking amongst the Jews. The pagans don't have the same Jewish expectations. So here, in a Jewish context, Jesus commands these disciples of his not to say a word.

Then he tries to reform their understanding of what *messiah* means. He says, "The Son of Man must suffer many things and be rejected by the elders, the chief priests and the teachers of the law, and he must be killed and on the third day be raised to life" (v. 22).

This seems pretty straightforward to us, but there is no way that Jesus's disciples understand these words at this time. Or, if they understand the words, they certainly don't believe them. The strongest proof of this assertion is that when Jesus is finally crucified, his disciples are shattered. When he is in the tomb, they are not secretly celebrating, breaking out joyful instruments, offering adoring worship to God, and saying: "Yes! Yes! We can hardly wait till Sunday!" They still do not have any category for a crucified and risen messiah. They haven't absorbed it.

Jesus doesn't let it rest there. He then says to them all, in effect, "By the way, not only am I going to the cross, but if you want to be my disciple, you must go too!" That is his meaning when he says, "Whoever wants to be my disciple must deny themselves and take up their cross daily and follow me" (9:23). Talk about not being very seeker-sensitive! "You want to be a Christian? Great! You'll need to be crucified." Oh, I know we have ways of domesticating the language a wee bit today. After all, for most of us, it does not mean actually getting nailed to or hung on a cross. It means death to self-interest and rising to newness of life. Even so, Jesus uses this extreme language because he is talking about an extreme death. Death to self is always painful—yet that's what it takes to become his disciple. While they are still thinking of triumphalism and earthly power, while they are doubtless entertaining secret thoughts about which one can be on his right hand and which one on his left in the kingdom, Jesus himself is focusing on his impending death by crucifixion. Jesus is God's Messiah, but this Messiah will suffer, die, and rise again.

Not Just Another Prophet

Second, Jesus stands in line with Israel's greatest God-endowed prophets, but he utterly outstrips them (Luke 9:28–36).

We know the account of the transfiguration. Two figures appear with Jesus: Moses, representing the onset of the law covenant, and Elijah, representing the onset of the prophetic age. These two men are talking about Jesus's "departure." The word literally means "exodus," a word choice designed to make us remember that all the Gospel writers are interested in showing how Jesus brings about a new exodus: an exodus out of sin that is the fulfillment of that earlier exodus out of slavery. But at the immediate level, Moses and Elijah are talking about Jesus's departure from this world or (to use the language of John's Gospel) his return to the Father with whom he had glory before the world began (John 17:5). In other words, they're talking about what will take place *in Jerusalem*. That's what the text says: "They spoke about his departure, which he was about to bring to fulfillment at Jerusalem" (Luke 9:31).

Never slow to stick his foot in his mouth, Peter says: "Master, it is good for us to be here. Let us put up three shelters—one for you, one for Moses and one for Elijah" (v. 33). Doubtless he thinks he is honoring Jesus. Peter is reasoning things out in his mind along these lines: "Moses is a hero from the past and Elijah was pretty spectacular too (just remember all those miracles!), and we would like to include you too, Jesus, because we have come to the conclusion that you belong to the same small group of spiritual elites." Peter has no idea how impossibly wrong he is.

When I was a boy in Quebec, the English Bible that all of us used was the King James Version, and the French Bible that all of us used was the Louis Segond. Both of them were somewhat old-fashioned—the English one more so than the French one. So all of my early Bible memory work was from the King James Version in English or from the Segond in French. My father was a formidable Bible memory man: he had thousands of lines of text stored in his memory—in English, in French, sometimes in Greek, and occasionally in Hebrew. When he wanted to tell us something, very often he would quote various biblical lines. Sometimes he ripped them out of their context, not because he didn't know the context, but because these were the categories that he used to express his thought. He thought in biblical language—in King James-ese, so to speak. So if we started complaining about the weather, he might say: "This is the day the Lord hath made. We will rejoice and be glad in it" (Ps. 118:24 KJV). And if we started spouting off about things we really did not understand (which, I'm sure, was pretty often), he would say, "He wist not what to say, so he said" (Mark 9:6 KJV; cf. Luke 9:33).

That is exactly what Peter is doing here: he does not have a clue what to say, so he speaks, and speaks inanities. When we do not have a clue what to say, the wisest thing in the world is to keep quiet. As the old adage puts it, "Better to keep silent and be thought a fool than to open your mouth and remove all doubt." Peter really does not understand who Jesus is, and God does not let him off the hook. A voice speaks from heaven, "*This* is my Son, whom I have chosen; listen to him" (Luke 9:35). God does not say this about Moses. God does not say this about Elijah. But he says it about Jesus.

The uses of the word *son* in the Bible are very diverse. Sometimes sonship is bound up with Davidic kingship: whenever a new son in David's line came to the throne, God said, in essence: "Today, I have begotten you. I will be your father and you will be my son." Because the king was supposed to so replicate God's reign, justice, truth, and integrity, he represented God as God's son, as it were.

Sometimes *son* refers to Israel collectively; sometimes to individual Israelites; once to Adam as God's "son"; and sometimes to angels. But on occasion, sonship is bound up with what later would be called the doctrine of the Trinity. The second person of the Godhead is referred to as "the Son of God." And sometimes sonship, as applied to Jesus, is bound up with the incarnation of the eternal Son. Luke 1:35 tells us that the Holy Spirit so comes upon Mary that the holy thing to be born of her will be called the Son of God.

Moses doesn't qualify. Elijah doesn't qualify. Jesus is still the misunderstood Messiah. The disciples themselves, the privileged three, still do not understand. As long as they can lump Jesus into the same grouping that embraces Moses and Elijah, the disciples do not grasp the utter uniqueness of Jesus. But the readers understand. By the time Luke puts these matters down on paper, Christians, living on the far side of Jesus's death and resurrection, understand perfectly well that Jesus cannot be compared with anyone else.

All of this is in support of a major point: in his own time, Jesus is the misunderstood Messiah, but Luke's readers see what Jesus's contemporaries did not see. Jesus is resolved to go to Jerusalem to die and rise again.

Not Eager to Linger

Third, Jesus alone has total power over the sick and the demonic, but he is about to depart (Luke 9:37–43a).

To see the power of the opening verses of this passage, you must read it without verse 41. Begin with the father's plea in verse 38: "Teacher, I beg you to look at my son, for he is my only child"—a desperate plea for help. Then verse 40: "I begged your disciples to drive it out, but they could not"—the incapacity of Jesus's disciples to provide help. Now skip verse 41 and read verse 42: "Even while the boy was coming, the demon threw him to the ground in a convulsion. But Jesus rebuked the impure spirit, healed the boy and gave him back to his father." In other words, in line with the first part of my third assertion, Jesus alone has total power over the sick and the demonic.

But in verse 41, Luke throws in some fascinating words of Jesus: "You unbelieving and perverse generation, how long shall I stay with you and put up with you? Bring your son here." In context, the "unbelieving and perverse generation" to which Jesus refers *includes the disciples.*

There are many texts in the New Testament that provide amazing insights into Jesus's contemplative reflections. This text is one of them. A fair reading shows that Jesus had a really hard time being with us. I am not referring to the challenge of the cross. In this passage, Jesus is interacting with his disciples, who, despite the fact that he has given them authority to cast out demons, really have very little faith. He has given them authority to heal the sick, but their authority seems to extend only to easy cases. When a hard case comes along, they panic and then turn tail. They are scared. They do not have much confidence after all; their faith is not very deep. Jesus finds this not only disturbing, but wretchedly unpleasant. He says, in effect: "You are a wicked and perverse generation. You have no idea how difficult it is to stay with you. I'm really looking forward to going home." Even though he knows that the way he goes home to his heavenly Father is via Jerusalem and the cross and resurrection, Jesus is eager to return to the glory that he had with the Father before the world began. Jesus alone has total power over the sick and the demonic, but he is about to depart.

Not a Power Broker

Fourth, Jesus again announces that he is about to die—and makes it clear why self-absorbed people cannot be loyal to him (Luke 9:43b–50).

Jesus says: "'Listen carefully to what I am about to tell you: The Son of Man is going to be delivered into the hands of men.' But they did not understand what this meant. It was hidden from them, so that they did not grasp it and they were afraid to ask him about it"

(vv. 44–45). Perhaps they do not want to expose their ignorance; doubtless they think that what he is saying has some really deep, deep meaning that is beyond them. But the most important reason why they cannot get it is given in the next verse (46): they are thinking in terms of greatness. While he is talking about his impending death, they are having an argument about which of them will be the greatest in the kingdom. This paragraph is parallel to the account we find in Matthew 20:20–28. Zebedee's wife comes to Jesus and says, "Please, could James and John sit on your left and on your right when you come into your kingdom?"

Clearly, the apostles are not focusing on death at all, still less on destruction and persecution. So when Jesus says these things, they assume he is talking in some subtle, symbol-laden, metaphorical fashion that finally escapes them. They think they already fully understand what messiahship and kingship are about—and what they think they understand tells them it is high time to get on the ladder and climb to the top along with Jesus. After all, there are twelve apostles, and they cannot all be at the top, you know. They are certainly not clamoring to join Jesus in his suffering.

So "Jesus, knowing their thoughts, took a little child and had him stand beside him" (Luke 9:47). Now, in some other passages, we are told to receive Jesus as a child does, that is, in simplicity. But look at the particular twist in Jesus's words here: "Whoever welcomes this little child in my name welcomes me; and whoever welcomes me welcomes the one who sent me. For it is the one who is least among you all who is the greatest" (v. 48).

They want to be close to Jesus, because they esteem Jesus to be great and becoming greater. But Jesus says, in effect, "I want to see how you welcome a child." If you welcome a child, you are not intent on scrambling up a bureaucratic ladder to the top of officialdom. You are not burnishing your resume in order to become secretary of state. The passage is not saying that Jesus is a mere cipher who can be confused with a child. That's not the point. Instead of sucking up to Jesus in order to be associated with someone who has power, they ought to be happy to receive a little child. They completely misunderstand.

Verse 49 makes a similar point: "'Master,' said John, 'we saw someone driving out demons in your name and we tried to stop him, because he is not one of us.'" How pathetic is that! They not only want to climb up the ladder to establish who among the Twelve will be minister of defense and who will be secretary of state in the kingdom, but they also want to crush any party that might provide any competition in this religion business. There might be some other people out there who have some connection with messianic hope, and Jesus's disciples do not want them to play the game at all. Sadly, the disciples do not even raise the question as to whether the other group is doing any good, speaking the truth, healing the sick, or doing any real life-transforming work. They are not thinking in terms of ministry, service, or fruitfulness. They are thinking about the scramble for power.

This is why self-absorbed people cannot truly grasp who Jesus is, why they cannot be loyal to him. Jesus remains the misunderstood Messiah as he trudges along the road to Jerusalem.

Not an Avenger
Fifth, Jesus heads toward Jerusalem to be killed, but he forbids killing the Samaritans who do not welcome him (Luke 9:51–56).

Jesus now explicitly discloses his resolve to go to Jerusalem to accomplish his "exodus," but any reader of Luke's Gospel knows that this departure is by way of the cross and the resurrection. In some ways, this is a relief for him. He is leaving a rather messy, sinful, and unbelieving situation behind. At another level, his resolve to go to Jerusalem entails spectacular anticipation. He will return to the glory that he had with the Father before the world began (to use the language of John 17:5). At still another level, this resolution brings raw terror, for it brings him to Gethsemane and Golgotha: "Father, if you are willing, take this cup from me" (Luke 22:42). But nothing will weaken his resolve to head to Jerusalem.

So why are the Samaritans introduced here? What does this brief narrative have to do with anything? Geographically, if Jesus is in the north and is heading south to Jerusalem, he can avoid crossing through Samaritan territory by slipping across the Jordan River and heading down the East Bank. Of course, it's more direct to go through Samaria, and that is what he does. But when he wants a little help along the way, the Samaritans do not want to provide any because he is going to Jerusalem. There is no love lost between Jews and Samaritans, but the Samaritans' reluctance to provide the courtesies that are offered to most strangers springs from more than racial antipathy. Jesus is going to Jerusalem for the Passover, one of the great Jewish feasts. The Samaritans do not want to support anybody who is going to Jerusalem and its temple for the Jewish feasts. The Samaritans utterly reject any authority from the temple. As far as they are concerned, the legitimate books of the Old Testament end with Deuteronomy. All the later material about David, Jerusalem, and kingship was, they believe, not given by God, but added to the Pentateuch by avaricious Jews who wanted to consolidate religious power for themselves. The Samaritans feel they have the true religion—it is just based on the Pentateuch. They had built their own temple in the area of Gerizim and Ebal, so no trips to Jerusalem for them. Relations between Jews and Gentiles were so bad about a century and a half earlier that the Jews invaded Samaritan territory and destroyed their temple. So when the Samaritans see that Jesus is heading for Jerusalem, they have nothing to do with him.

Jesus's disciples, full of loyal zeal, suggest that they should call down fire from heaven to wipe out these wretches. After all, Jesus is the true Messiah! He is the promised King! Elisha called down fire from heaven just for being called "Baldy!" (2 Kings 2:23), and surely the Samaritans' offense is greater than that. Wouldn't the destruction of the Samaritans be justified?

They do not foresee, of course, that when they arrive in Jerusalem, they will all abandon Jesus and flee, refusing to be identified with him, just like these Samaritans. All of them will distance themselves from Jesus—Peter with curses. Should Jesus kill the Samaritans? Okay, then, should he kill his disciples for the same sins? Of course, when Jesus arrives in Jerusalem to die, instead of the Samaritans, instead of the disciples, everything will be turned on its head. When he gets to Jerusalem, crowds will cry: "Crucify him! Crucify him!" Should he call down fire on them too? It was my sin that held him there on the cross. Should he call down fire on me? And the answer to all those questions is—yes. On one level, he should. To reject the incarnate God-man, who is heading to Jerusalem to give his life—what terrible blasphemy is that?

But Jesus does not let it happen; he does not call down fire from heaven on the Samaritans. He does not call down fire from heaven on his disciples. Why not? Because he is resolved to go to Jerusalem, where he will die on the cross for sinners. In his own day, he is the perpetually misunderstood Messiah.

So here is this first point: in his own time, Jesus is the misunderstood Messiah, but Luke's readers see what Jesus's contemporaries do not. Jesus is resolved to go to Jerusalem to die and rise again.

But there is a second crucial point that is established by Jesus's resolve to head to Jerusalem. I shall tell you what it is, and then we shall scan three ensuing passages to make the point clear.

The Clarifying Cross

In his own time, Jesus is the misunderstood Messiah, but Luke's readers see, as Jesus's contemporaries do not, how everything that takes place in Jesus's life is clarified because it falls under the shadow of the impending cross.

Let me show you how this works out.

Cross-Carrying Disciples

First, begin with the next little section, 9:57–62. There are three men who either want to follow Jesus or who are challenged to do so. The first says, "I will follow you wherever you go" (v. 57). Oh, good: baptize him and get him to tell his testimony. But Jesus replies, "Foxes have dens and birds have nests, but the Son of Man has no place to lay his head" (v. 58). Jesus says to another man, "Follow me," but the man replies, "Lord, first let me go and bury my father" (v. 59)—which, in Jesus's view, disqualifies him. The third man Jesus dismisses on similar grounds, and concludes, "No one who puts a hand to the plow and looks back is fit for service in the kingdom of God" (v. 62).

If you read through these verses in a straightforward manner that largely ignores the flow of Luke's Gospel, you can still make a lot of sense of them. Jesus turns away would-be disciples, even invited would-be disciples, who are halfhearted or unwilling to face certain costs. In Bibles that have outlines in them, this passage is often titled, "The Cost of Being a Disciple." But now read the passage again, this time remembering that Jesus speaks these words *as he is on his way to Jerusalem and the cross*. What does this perspective add? Immediately we perceive that these verses do not constitute a merely abstract reflection on the nature of the cost of discipleship. Rather, what is in view is the cost of following a Savior who goes to the cross on our behalf. The only adequate response to such self-sacrifice is unqualified devotion: we must follow him with our own self-death; we must take up our crosses and follow him.

Heaven-Inscribed Names

Second, consider Luke 10:1–20, a passage that is really quite moving. Jesus commissions a number of followers, seventy or seventy-two, to engage in kingdom work, and they come back thoroughly delighted with the results: "Lord, even the demons submit to us in your name," they say (v. 17). He replies: "I saw Satan fall like lightning from heaven. I have given you authority to trample on snakes and scorpions and to overcome all the power of the enemy; nothing will harm you. However, do not rejoice that the spirits submit to you, but rejoice that your names are written in heaven" (vv. 18–20).

The meaning of the passage, taken on its own without worrying too much about the flow of thought in Luke's Gospel, is pretty straightforward. Your identity is not bound up with your ministry; it is bound up with your election: "Your names are written in heaven." Many of us in ministry spend a great deal of our lives struggling with the ferocious giant called envy, as we foolishly tie our identities and significance to the scope of our ministries, and then resent those who are more fruitful. But Jesus insists we are to rejoice because our names are written in heaven, not because of our fruitfulness in ministry. The passage is clear enough, and very powerful.

Nevertheless, the passage becomes even more powerful when we remember that Jesus says these words on the way to Jerusalem. In the light of the fact that Jesus is resolved to wend his way to the cross, the words "rejoice that your names are written in heaven" take on an additional significance. On what basis have their names been secured in heaven? They are secured because Jesus is on the way to the cross. The disciples are mandated to rejoice because Jesus's atoning death is precisely what secures their place in heaven. The spectacular grace they have received, so much more important than mere power in ministry, is tied immovably to Jesus's resolution to go to Jerusalem. While they are being slightly triumphalistic about their own ministry, Jesus is going to the cross to secure their salvation.

The Ultimate Good Samaritan

Third, what shall we say about the parable of the good Samaritan (10:25–37)? In some circles, this parable means nothing more than this: if you want to be a Christian, love your neighbor as yourself. Doesn't Jesus end by saying, "Go and do likewise" (v. 37)? Some believe this is what it means to be a Christian. For some interpreters, this is how you *become* a Christian.

As was the case with the last two passages we scanned, we must first read the passage closely before asking ourselves what additional light is shed on it when we recall that Jesus tells this

parable *on his way to Jerusalem and the cross.* The parable is struc-
tured in two dialogues. In each of these dialogues, the lawyer asks
a question; Jesus responds not with an answer, but with his own
question; the lawyer answers Jesus's question; and Jesus finally
answers the lawyer's question.

Look closely, beginning with verse 25: "Teacher, what must I
do to inherit eternal life?" That's the initial question, the question
posed by the expert in the law. Jesus answers with his own question: "What is written in the Law? How do you read it?" The expert
in the law answers Jesus's question with two biblical texts: "Love
the Lord your God with all your heart and with all your soul and
with all your strength and with all your mind" and "Love your
neighbor as yourself." Only then does Jesus answer the lawyer's
initial question: "You have answered correctly. Do this and you
will live" (v. 28).

When Jesus says, "Do this and you will live," some readers take
him to mean something like this: "Go ahead. That's how you get
saved. Do this and you will live." But that is certainly not how this
man understands Jesus's words. It is important to remember that
on another occasion, Jesus himself quotes the same two passages to
which the lawyer appeals, but when he does so, it is in an entirely
different context. Read the account in Mark 12:28–34. A different
lawyer there asks Jesus what are the two greatest commandments of
the law. Jesus replies, in effect, "The first is love God with all your
heart, soul, mind, and strength (Deuteronomy 6), and the second
is love your neighbor as yourself (Leviticus 19)." In other words,
when Jesus quotes these passages, he is not answering the question:
"How do I get into heaven? How do I inherit the kingdom? How
do I finally secure salvation?" Rather, he is answering the question, "What is the greatest commandment in the law?" The lawyer
in our passage in Luke 10 quotes these two Old Testament texts to
argue that the way you inherit eternal life, the basis on which you
are accepted by God, is by obeying these two laws: love God with
your heart, soul, mind, and strength, and love your neighbor as

yourself. So Jesus replies, in effect: "Brilliant answer. Go ahead. That's all you have to do to get in."

Does anyone you know genuinely love God with all his heart, soul, mind, and strength? On rare occasions, we might love our neighbors as ourselves, but even then we ruin it by patting ourselves on the back for doing so. Does anyone you know genuinely love her neighbor as herself? If those are the conditions for getting in, no one is getting in: we are all damned. In other words, when Jesus says, "You have answered correctly. Do this and you will live," he is exposing the man's utter folly. The lawyer's lack of realism, his lack of self-understanding, is frankly appalling. That is why Jesus says, in effect: "Are you serious? Go ahead. Try it. If you succeed, you're in." Realization dawns; the man knows he's been nobbled. That is why he seeks to justify himself (Luke 10:29).

This desire to justify himself prompts him to ask another question, thus initiating the second dialogue: "And who is my neighbor?" he asks (v. 29). Once again, Jesus does not immediately answer the expert's question, but asks his own question. In order to set up his question, Jesus tells the parable of the good Samaritan: A man was going down from Jerusalem to Jericho; he was attacked, robbed, beaten up, and left for dead; and three different men came upon him lying by the road and displayed various responses to his misery. Once Jesus has finished the parable, he asks his question: "Which of these three do you think was a neighbor to the man who fell into the hands of robbers?" The expert in the law replies, "The one who had mercy on him." Jesus tells him, "Go and do likewise," and thus, the second dialogue comes to an end.

One of the minor themes in Luke's Gospel is self-justification. It is worth pausing to think about that. In the Bible, justification is that act by which God declares guilty people to be just because of the action of another, namely Christ Jesus, who bore our sins in his body on the tree. That's justification. God declares sinners to be just. Self-justification occurs when sinners declare themselves to be just: they justify themselves.

That is what the expert in the law is doing with his question. He wants to justify himself to prove that he is really just; perhaps he really is good enough to inherit eternal life.

Attempts at self-justification keep recurring in Luke's Gospel. For example, in Luke 16, Jesus talks a while about money. Then Luke tells us: "The Pharisees, who loved money, heard all this and were sneering at Jesus. He said to them, 'You are the ones *who justify yourselves in the eyes of others*, but God knows your hearts. What people value highly is detestable in God's sight'" (vv. 14–15). In other words, they are justifying themselves on the basis of their wealth: "God must love me and accept me since he has blessed me with a wonderful amount of money."

Then, in Luke 18, we find the parable of the Pharisee and the tax collector:

> To some who were confident of their own righteousness [that is, they justified themselves] and looked down on everyone else, Jesus told this parable: "Two men went up to the temple to pray, one a Pharisee and the other a tax collector. The Pharisee stood by himself and prayed: 'God, I thank you that I am not like other people—robbers, evildoers, adulterers—or even like this tax collector. I fast twice a week and give a tenth of all I get.'
>
> "But the tax collector stood at a distance. He would not even look up to heaven, but beat his breast and said, 'God, have mercy on me, a sinner.'" (vv. 9–13)

And what does Jesus say? "I tell you that this man, rather than the other, went home *justified* before God" (v. 14). One man justifies himself, but it doesn't win anything. His self-justification is part of what condemns him. The other man is justified by God. And this justification is all that counts.

The lawyer in our passage in Luke 10 belongs to those who justify themselves. That is why he asks his further question. And that is why Jesus exposes the man's pathetic excuses. After narrating the parable of the good Samaritan, Jesus, as we've seen, asks this question: "Which of these three do you think was a neighbor to the man who fell into the hands of robbers?" (v. 36). While the man wants to ask, "Who is my neighbor?" so as to make excuses for himself, Jesus exposes the man's moral bankruptcy by asking a different question: "To whom are you the neighbor?"

So the parable of the good Samaritan is fairly straightforward. But now we must reflect on the fact that Jesus tells this parable on his way to Jerusalem, on his way to the cross. Who is the ultimate good Samaritan? As Jesus tells the story, the good Samaritan is a figure who looks after a broken and bruised unknown man who has been left for dead at the side of the road. The Samaritan owes this injured man nothing, but he risks his life for him, spends his own wealth to look after him, and provides him with a ride while he himself walks. Moreover, because he pays for his expenses on an open-ended account, he saves this poor wretch from slavery. Under the laws of the day, if the man cannot pay the innkeeper for the further weeks of care (And how could he? He had been robbed of everything, including his clothes.), he will have no choice but to sell himself into slavery to the innkeeper because he cannot discharge the debt. The Samaritan's generosity saves the man not only from death but from slavery. So again we ask the question: Outside the narrative world of the parable, who is the good Samaritan? Who acts this way?

If you ask that question while remembering that Jesus is on the way to the cross, it looks a little different. Who is the ultimate good Samaritan who comes to broken people, who, if left alone, will certainly die? Who binds up their wounds, saves their lives, and frees them forever from slavery, paying for all of it? You simply cannot fail to see that the ultimate good Samaritan is this Jesus who is on the way to Jerusalem—precisely *because* he is on the way to Jerusalem. Now that is not Jesus's point when he tells the parable of the good Samaritan. But Luke has so configured the parable in the portion of his Gospel that reports Jesus's resolution to go to Jerusalem that you cannot fail to see that this is the case.

In his own time, Jesus is the misunderstood Messiah, but Luke's readers see, as Jesus's contemporaries do not, how everything that takes place in Jesus's life is clarified because it falls under the shadow of the impending cross.

A Life Aimed toward Jerusalem

I conclude:

First, away with all attempts to drive a wedge between Jesus's teaching on the one hand and his death and resurrection on the other. For a long time, books have been written with titles like *The Teaching of Jesus*, *The Teaching of Jesus in the Synoptic Gospels*, or *The Teaching of Jesus in Luke*. Such books begin with the author telling us something like this: "In this book, I am not going to talk about the passion narrative. I'm not going to mention the cross and resurrection. I'm going to focus exclusively on the teaching of Jesus." Without exception, such books distort the teaching of Jesus, for when you read the Gospels carefully, you discover that Jesus teaches with the cross in view. That is why some wag has said the four Gospels are essentially passion narratives with extended introductions. In no Gospel is this more obvious than in Luke. Jesus expresses his resolve to go to the cross—and all of his teaching has to be put under the looming shadow of the impending cross. If you try to present the teaching of Jesus by itself, stripped of what it points to, you end up with a great deal of moralism that sadly overlooks the cross and resurrection toward which all four canonical Gospels are rushing.

Second, away also with all attempts to say that Luke is not much interested in the atonement. Many commentators say this. They may point to the fact that Luke does not have a parallel to Mark 10:45 (cf. Matt. 20:28), which states clearly that Jesus came "to give his life as a ransom for many." Yet Luke preserves many ways of focusing on the cross, and one of the most dramatic is the way in which Jesus resolutely sets his face to Jerusalem. And when he reaches Jerusalem, during his final meal before the cross, he breaks the bread and takes the cup, insisting that this cup is the new covenant in his blood, which is shed for many for the remission of sins. This book has its own way of being saturated with the atonement.

Third, and above all, we cannot rightly read Luke's Gospel without reflecting long and hard on the christological implications of Jesus's resolve to head to Jerusalem. Are you among those who think Jesus was a fine man, but no more? Or perhaps even a fine prophet, but no more? Luke will not allow you to read Jesus this way, and if you try to do so, you will end up with self-justification and you will die. In reality, Jesus is resolved to go to Jerusalem, and you cannot know the real Jesus without seeing him on the cross and seeing him emerge from the empty tomb.

Or are you among those who think of Jesus in merely therapeutic terms? Jesus becomes a bit like the man from the TV commercial for Britain's Automobile Association: Jesus is a nice man; he's a very nice man; he's a very, very, very nice man. And when you break down, he comes along and fixes you. And so all the focus is on you and your brokenness. But the real Jesus, the historical Jesus, is resolved to go to Jerusalem. His fixing of people is radical. He goes to the cross, bears their sins, and pours out his transforming Spirit on them, commanding them and enabling them to take up their crosses and follow him.

> There is a fountain filled with blood,
> Drawn from Immanuel's veins;
> And sinners plunged beneath that flood,
> Lose all their guilty stains.[2]

> My hope is built on nothing less
> Than Jesus' blood and righteousness.
> I dare not trust the sweetest frame,
> But wholly lean on Jesus' name.[3]

Jesus resolved to go to Jerusalem.

---

[2] From the hymn "There Is a Fountain Filled with Blood" by William Cowper, 1771.
[3] From the hymn "My Hope Is Built on Nothing Less" by Edward Mote, 1834.

5

JESUS AND THE LOST

Luke 15:1–32

Kevin DeYoung

Before church one Sunday, a deacon asked me how I was feeling about the sermon. As a preacher, I never really feel good about my sermons before, during, or after, so I told him I wasn't feeling all that great. "Well, Kevin," he said, "it's Luke 15. Even if you're way off, it's still going to be pretty good." He was right—about the text, I mean. You can hardly go wrong with Luke 15.

I'd like to look at this familiar passage, with its three familiar parables, in three ways. First, we'll consider one thing we need to understand, then two things we learn about God, and finally three things we ought to do as a result.

Context Is King

The one thing we need to understand is the *context*. Throughout his Gospel, Luke employs a pattern by which some event or question prompts Jesus to give an extended speech, often in the form of a parable. In Luke 10, for example, a lawyer asks Jesus, "What shall I do to inherit eternal life?" (v. 25). Jesus tells him that he must love God with all of his heart, soul, strength, and mind, and love his neighbor as himself (vv. 27–28). Being a good lawyer, the man responds with another question: "And who is my neighbor?" (v. 29). Jesus then gives an answer out of this context by telling the story of the good Samaritan (vv. 30–37).

In Luke 12, the context is an argument about a contested inheritance between squabbling brothers. When someone shouts from the crowd for Jesus to settle the matter, he reminds them that "one's life does not consist in the abundance of his possessions" (v. 15). He then expands on this statement by telling the crowds the parable of the rich fool (vv. 16–21).

Likewise, in Luke 14:7, we get the context right at the beginning: "Now he told a parable to those who were invited, when he noticed how they chose the places of honor." Jesus notices that everyone at the feasts and banquets rushes to sit up front—unlike people arriving for church! This prompts Jesus to tell the parable of the wedding feast (vv. 8–11).

Over and over, Luke helps his audience by introducing the parables with important background information. He does this again at the beginning of chapter 15: "The tax collectors and sinners were all drawing near to hear him. And the Pharisees and the scribes grumbled" (vv. 1–2). The Jewish leaders have little patience for sinners and tax collectors, and even less for popular teachers who think nothing of fraternizing with them. Jesus should know better—at least that's what the scribes and Pharisees think.

Sinners is a general term. It can mean the common people, the non-Pharisees, or those who don't follow the Pharisaic traditions. It can refer to those who are ritually unclean, those not fastidious in keeping the Law of Moses, or simply those who are not walking in God's ways. The term is broad enough to include all of these ideas. The sinners are those violating the acceptable standards of Jewish conduct—whether in the eyes of the Pharisees or in the eyes of God. They are bad Jews, hardly considered real Jews at all.

Tax collectors is a narrower category and one requiring a little more explanation. Tax collectors are not well loved today, and they were even less appreciated in first-century Palestine. The common person hated tax collectors, and for good reason. By the time of

Christ, the Roman Empire did not do its own tax collection. Instead, Rome farmed out the responsibility. The process for winning the job was much like winning a public-works contract today. A group of tax collectors—a kind of investment firm—would submit a bid to pay the people's taxes to Rome for one year in advance. The winners of the contract would then pay the agreed-upon amount to Rome and would be empowered to collect taxes and to recoup their investment. Whatever they collected on top of that, of course, would line their own pockets.

The problem was not taxes per se, or even that the collectors made a profit. The problem was that invariably the tax collectors made a profit by cheating and swindling. Tax collection was a very subjective enterprise. The collectors would set up booths along the roads, and as people would come through, the value of their goods would be assessed, a tax rate would be applied, and that was that. There was no recourse, no board of appeal, no way to get justice if you were treated unfairly.

And you probably were. Tax collectors could confiscate goods. They made false accusations. They threatened. They could determine the value of your goods. And because no one knew the tax rates, they could determine those too. With mighty Rome in their corner, tax collectors could do just about whatever they pleased. They were like the corrupt city bosses from the last century or some kind of state-sponsored mafia.

Above all, tax collectors were liars, cheaters, and swindlers. The *Mishnah*, a Jewish document from a century or so after the time of Jesus, often mentions thieves, robbers, and tax collectors in the same breath. They could not be judges or witnesses in court. They could not enter the synagogue. Rabbis could declare a house unclean if a tax collector entered it. Both the liberal and conservative wings of Judaism agreed that it was acceptable to lie to tax collectors. Every good person knew that tax collectors were no good.

And here you have Jesus not only ministering to them, but also receiving them. He eats with them and seems to be at ease in their presence.

It would be one thing to see your pastor at Starbucks engaged in obvious ministry with a bunch of notorious sinners from your community. You'd think: "There's my pastor reaching out to the lost, buying them coffee on the church credit card, doing an evangelistic Bible study. Terrific." It would be quite another thing to knock at a fraternity house door as you're selling candy bars for the marching band and see your pastor inside playing cards with loud music blaring. Or worse yet, to see him leaving the abortion clinic you're picketing and hear him yell back through the open door to one of the doctors: "Hey, my place. Seven o'clock, right? Looking forward to it!"

Imagine the people you most revere and respect sharing a meal with the atheist scientist, the predatory attorney, or the sleazy mayor. Imagine your holy role models sitting down to eat with whatever category of sinner you have—those on the wrong side of the political aisle, prostitutes, IRS agents, the filthy rich, the dirty poor. Might you find it hard not to murmur, at least a little?

The Pharisees see Jesus eating with sinners and tax collectors, and they grumble. What is he doing, they wonder, enjoying life and having a good time with people like that?

Indeed, what is he doing? That's the problem that prompts these three parables. This is the background we need to understand about this passage.

Our Redeeming and Rejoicing God

In each of the parables in chapter 15, Jesus introduces us to a main character. First, in verse 4, "What *man* of you, having a hundred sheep . . . ?" Then, in verse 8, "Or what *woman*, having ten silver coins . . . ?" And again in verse 11, "There was a *man* who had two sons. . . ." The point is not to say that God is a shepherd, a woman, or a father. Rather, Jesus is comparing their attitudes and actions with God's attitudes and actions. If a shepherd is like this, if a woman is like this, and if a father is like this, how much more is God like this?

So what do we learn about God in Luke 15? Two things.

First, we learn that *God seeks and saves*. We see this clearly in each of the parables.

1. Jesus begins with the shepherd—strong, tender, seeking the stray. The parable is reminiscent of Isaiah 40 and the divine shepherd who gently carries the nursing lambs, holds them close, and brings them to safety. Our God is active in searching out those who are lost.

In my neighborhood, on almost every light pole, there are signs for lost dogs or cats. When I first noticed these signs, I felt a tinge of sympathy—for the dogs anyway (the cats probably wanted out). But nothing seemed to happen. The seasons changed. The pictures grew faded because of the weather. And yet, many of the signs are still up today. I can't help but wonder: Is anyone actually looking for these animals? Do they expect me to do all the work? Did the owners just put up signs and assume the pets would read them, realize they're missing, and saunter on home?

This is not the way God seeks. The shepherd doesn't just put up a sign that says, "Hey, I lost a sheep." He leaves the ninety-nine behind and goes after the one who is missing.

2. In the second parable, Jesus tells the story of a woman who loses one of her coins—a drachma, equivalent to a denarius or a day's wage. She doesn't wait for the coin to come to her. She lights a lamp and sweeps the house. She seeks diligently until she finds it.

This woman searches for what is lost like a mom, not like a child. I have kids. I know how this goes. One of my boys will come to me and say, "Dad, did you find my iPod?"

And I'll say something like: "We got you an iPod? What were we thinking?"

Then he'll say, "Come on, Dad!"

And I'll say, "Okay, where did you look?"

"I . . . I looked on my bed."

"We have more places in the house than your bed. Why don't you look somewhere else?"

"Well, I can't find it. Can you find it?"

"No, you look for it."

"Why don't you look for it?"

"Am I your iPod's keeper?"

Then I go downstairs and see the iPod sitting on the couch, middle cushion, dead center. "Did you look here?" I ask.

"I didn't think to look *there*."

Kids don't know how to search, but moms do. And they expect everyone else to know how to find things like they do.

My wife sometimes plays a trick on me. During the summer, when it's hot and humid, and my fingers get a little sticky, I'll take off my wedding ring at night and put it on the nightstand. In the morning, if I forget to put it back on, my wife will hide it and just watch.

"Honey," I say, "where's my ring?"

"I don't know," she says sheepishly.

"You took it, didn't you?"

"No, I didn't. I don't know where it is. But I know where *my* ring is because I love you."

Of course, she knows where my ring is, but she wants me to look for it. She wants to see that I'm sorry to have lost something so valuable and precious. She wants me to seek it out, to go and find it. She wants me to sweep the house like the woman in Jesus's parable.

3. In the third story, we meet a father. This parable is more complicated, so we need to be careful. We don't want to overinterpret parables and try to make every detail teach some lesson. I suppose someone could argue that the example in this parable is different because the father never actually goes out and searches for the son. But that would miss the point. The point is that while the son is still a long way off, the father sees him, is filled with compassion, runs to him, throws his arms around him, and kisses his cheek. Like this father, God welcomes home his children. He seeks out prodigals and profligates.

And he's seeking people in our cities. The university town where I minister is in one of Michigan's more liberal counties. Our church has several hundred members, a nice size but nothing enormous. Our growth has been slow and deliberate. No great revival has broken out. It's tempting to think that there aren't many more people left in our area who are looking for a church. That may be true, but God is still looking for sinners here! There is One seeking out the lost more than any of us. That ought to give us patience and it ought to give us love for those who seem (or feel) the most unlovable. Perhaps that person in your life who is so frustrating, so belligerent, or so opposed to everything you stand for is the lost coin God is searching for or the lost sheep that he has left the ninety-nine to go and find.

You may wonder, what is the mission of Jesus? What was the purpose of his ministry here on earth? How you answer this question will profoundly shape the priorities of your life and your church. Did Jesus come to make people nicer? To get people to recycle? To get a candidate elected? What was his mission? Fortunately, we don't have to wonder. Jesus answers the question himself. In Luke 5, Jesus is eating a meal with Levi, a tax collector whom Jesus has just called to be a disciple. Right on cue, the Pharisees and scribes grumble and wag their fingers at Jesus. But listen to his reply: "I have not come to call the righteous but sinners to repentance" (v. 32).

That is what Jesus is about. That is his mission.

We find a similar story in Luke 19. Zacchaeus, who is one of these tax collectors, climbs a tree to get a better view of Jesus passing by. But Jesus doesn't just pass by. Instead, he stops and invites himself to Zacchaeus's house, where the tax collector "receive[s] him joyfully" (v. 6). Zacchaeus then states publicly that he will give half of his possessions to the poor and pay back four times what he's swindled. He never prays a sinner's prayer, but his heart is obviously transformed. Jesus, knowing this, announces, "Salvation has come to this house" (v. 9). Then Jesus adds this summary of his purpose: "The Son of Man came to seek and to save the lost" (v. 10).

That was the mission of Jesus—which means the church better have a category of lostness. We talk about the unchurched, the underchurched, and the dechurched, and all of these terms have a place. But let us not forget this biblical category: lost. People are lost and need to be found.

This is a scandalous thing, a hard part of the Christian message for many people to swallow. You may be thinking: "I can't talk like Jesus does, not in my church. There are non-Christians there on Sunday. They don't want to hear they are lost. No one wants to be lost." It's wonderful if you have non-Christians at church and non-Christians in your life. We all should. But there comes a point, when given the opportunity or the text to expound, that we need to say: "Look, I understand this may be offensive, but I have to say what Jesus said. He's my Lord. He's *the* Lord. And he says clearly that people are lost without him."

The hard thing in our world is that lost people don't often know they're lost. Not too long ago, I was meeting up with friends for lunch at Wendy's. I got there on time, but no one else showed up. I kept waiting and waiting. It was frustrating. I thought: "Really? I'm the only one? No one else can tell time? No one else can find this place? Is everyone else lost?" But then I got a text message: "Hey, man, you coming? We're waiting on you." My friends had been there all along, waiting for me—at Burger King. I had been absolutely convinced that I was in the right place and that everyone else was lost. But it turned out that they were where they needed to be and I was the one missing. Is it possible that you or the people you love are convinced they are in the right place when in fact they are absolutely lost?

> Amazing grace, how sweet the sound,
> That saved a wretch like me.
> I once was lost, but now am found,
> Was blind, but now I see.[1]

We need a category for lostness, and we need a passion for seeking. This was the mission of Jesus. That's why he spent time with tax collectors and sinners. That's also what Jesus shows us about

---

[1] From the hymn "Amazing Grace" by John Newton, 1779.

God in these parables. Right now, in your church, in your school, in your city, God is seeking out sinners. And he will save some.

Second, we learn that *God not only seeks out sinners, he rejoices when he finds them.*

This is Jesus's singular point. He means to contrast the grumbling of the Pharisees and the scribes with the gladness of God. We see this in Luke 15:7: "Just so, I tell you, there will be more joy in heaven over one sinner who repents. . . ." Or again in verse 10: "Just so, I tell you, there is joy before the angels of God over one sinner who repents." And in verse 32: "It was fitting to celebrate and be glad, for this your brother was dead, and is alive; he was lost, and is found." Each parable in this chapter ends with the same divine joy.

And notice that this rejoicing goes public. In verse 6, after the shepherd returns, we read, "he calls together his friends and his neighbors, saying to them, 'Rejoice with me, for I have found my sheep that was lost.'" In verse 9, the woman "calls together her friends and neighbors, saying, 'Rejoice with me, for I have found the coin that I had lost.'" And in verses 22–23, the father says to his servants, in effect, "Bring the robe, put on the ring, get shoes on his feet, kill the fattened calf, let's eat and celebrate." The shepherd, the woman, and the father all celebrate—with friends, with neighbors, with servants. They know that there is something in the nature of joy that must overflow and must be shared with others.

The next time you're in a big group, take notice when something funny happens. When the laughing starts, there's an instinctive turning of the head. You look to make eye contact with someone else who is laughing. You search for a moment of mutual recognition that you might share the joy together. We can't help it. We are made to experience joy with others.

In these parables, we learn that God shares his joy with the angels. That's his community of holy mirth. And what does God rejoice over? He rejoices over contrition. He rejoices over the person who weeps for sin. He rejoices over those who turn from their own ways. The Bible calls this repentance, and we see it in all three parables. Verse 7: "there will be . . . joy in heaven over one sinner who repents." Verse 10: "there is joy before the angels of God over one sinner who repents." And in verses 18–19, the son rehearses his penitent speech: "Father, I have sinned against heaven and before you. I am no longer worthy to be called your son. Treat me as one of your hired servants." He accepts the consequences of his choices. He offers no excuses, only confession. He makes no claims, but only clings to the mercy of his father.

Repentance is absolutely delightful to God. It is as much an act of grace to repent as it is to not sin in the first place. That's because true, Spirit-wrought repentance, as opposed to mere regret, is a miracle of grace. Anyone can feel regret. Paul talks about this in 2 Corinthians 7, about the difference between worldly grief and godly grief. Worldly grief says: "Oh, man, I was caught. I was so embarrassed that I lost my job. My family's messed up. I lost face. I'm so ashamed." But godly grief is precious to God. Why? Because when you truly repent, you are saying before God and before the world: "I was wrong. God, you are right. I want your ways, not my ways. I trust you, not myself. I own all of my sins, and I look to you for everything that I lack." God delights in that.

You may think there is nothing commendable, nothing beautiful, nothing comely about you. But your repentance would be oh so sweet to your heavenly Father. He would smile to see your restoration. He would delight in his sheep returning to the fold, his coin returning to its place, his child coming home.

I was working on this passage one Saturday when my oldest son, who was nine years old at the time, texted me a message: "Dad, can you come home?"

I said, "Sorry, I'm working on a sermon."

He said, "Well, I could help you."

I said, "Okay, read Luke 15 and write me up some thoughts."

And he did. I thought this line was pretty good: "It is not the same to have one out of two or ninety-nine out of a hundred or even nine out of ten, because it makes the biggest difference to have even one small thing missing."

I thought, "Yes, it does make a big difference to God to have even one small thing missing." And when that one person repents, there is great joy in heaven.

God is calling together the angels—Michael, Gabriel, and the thousands of others whose names we don't know. He's calling them to a party: come, celebrate, rejoice. Repentance is the opportunity for your own personal heavenly parade. I've been in a few parades—in the marching band a few times, and twice as the *domine* (i.e., pastor) on the Tulip Time float (ask me about it some time)—but I've never had my own parade. I've never had ticker tape just for me, fireworks just for me, music just for me. But that's the scene in heaven every time a sinner repents. And the Father, Son, and Holy Spirit, together with all the angels, never grow tired of it. There is nothing but more joy, more gladness, and more rejoicing every time another sinner repents.

So here's the logic: if the shepherd goes after a lost sheep, a woman looks for her lost coin, and a father welcomes home his lost son, how much more does God seek out the lost and rejoice when they are found? We have a God who seeks out sinners and absolutely revels in their return.

Be Mindful, Prepared, Marked

So what should we do as a result of what we've seen about our God? I have three applications.

First, *let us be mindful of the need for both relationships and repentance.* This is going to be a great challenge for the church in the years ahead. It won't be hard to have a church that's good at relationships. It won't be hard to have a church that's good at telling sinners to repent. What will be hard is to have people who, like Jesus, are full of relationships with outsiders and also bold to talk about repentance.

Jesus associated with sinners, but in a way that addressed the real issues of life. He never offered cheap grace. He did not participate in their sin or in any way condone it. And yet, he never apologized for being on the inside with outsiders. It was his mission. What kind of doctor refuses to see patients? What kind of farmer refuses to get his hands dirty? What kind of church has no room for sinners? People reviled Jesus and called him a glutton and a drunkard, a friend of tax collectors and sinners because he received people like this. There was something about Jesus that sinners found attractive and inviting.

As something of a public person, I've been called all sorts of things. I've had epithets and accusations hurled my way many times. But with all the names I've been called, I've never been charged with this: being a friend of tax collectors and sinners. I doubt many Christian have. The world is not saying, "Would you look at those folks, at those evangelicals; would you look at those Reformed folks—they are friends of sinners." And why not? Do we fear contamination more than we put confidence in Christ's power to cleanse?

Obviously we must have wisdom here. I'm not encouraging people with drinking problems to hang out in bars or new believers to keep doing the same old things. I'm not saying we should watch the worst and sleaziest movies and call that relevance. We don't want to swing to an ungodly extreme, but that's not the danger for most of us. One of the reasons evangelism is so hard for us is because we are friends with so few non-Christians. We must not look at outsiders as potential contagions, but as human beings made in God's image, as human beings in need of a Savior, and as human beings God can save.

Jesus associated with sinners and had warm relationships with them, but that never prevented him from talking about repentance. He did not call sinners to join him in despising the righteous. He did not call sinners to unfettered self-expression. He did not call sinners to eat, drink, and be merry (or, in our parlance, to eat, drink, and be tolerant). He called them to repentance. One commentator says, "Jesus neither condoned sin, left people in their sin, nor communicated any disdain for sinners."[2] He was not passive, just waiting

---

[2] Klyne R. Snodgrass, *Stories with Intent: A Comprehensive Guide to the Parables of Jesus* (Grand Rapids: Eerdmans, 2008), 116.

around for people to get their act together, and he was not passive about confronting sin. No one in the history of the world has been more inclusive of repentant sinners than Jesus, and no one has been more intolerant of sin. What's needed more than ever in our day is courage, the sort of courage that says, "I am not afraid to spend time with anyone, and I'm not afraid to tell anyone about sin." We see in these parables a Savior who has relationships with sinners, and a Savior who is unafraid to call those sinners to repentance.

Second, *let us be prepared to seek and find all kinds of lost people.* All kinds. It's widely understood that the final parable of Luke 15 is really about two sons. Though the story is usually called the parable of the prodigal son, it ought to be called the parable of the compassionate father and his two lost sons. Both sons are lost, each in his own way.

The younger brother's sin is easier to see. He leaves with his inheritance and squanders it in riotous living. He ends up in the worst possible place for a Jew, starving in the pen with unclean pigs. Maybe you used to be there. Maybe you are there, and God wants you to come to your senses and realize, "Surely, my Father has something better for me than wasting away waiting for a scrap from the swine."

Perhaps you see yourself in the parable. There are two Rembrandt paintings of the prodigal son. One is of the son returning, kneeling before the father. That's the more famous painting. But the other is also powerful. It's called *The Prodigal Son in the Tavern* or sometimes *The Prodigal Son in the Brothel*. It's a picture of a man sitting with a woman on his lap. The striking thing is that it's a self-portrait. Rembrandt painted his own face into the scene, along with that of his wife Saskia. If you know anything about Rembrandt, you know he was a sinner. But in that moment at least, he understood that the story of the prodigal son is not only about someone else, it's about him, about you, and about me.

And what about the older brother? His sin is not as obvious, but it is just as damning. In Luke 15:28, we see a surprising picture of physical distance. The younger brother, who squandered his inheritance, has returned and is now inside celebrating with his father. But the older brother, who has been the faithful insider for all of his life, is now on the outside looking in.

The older brother wants justice from the father instead of mercy. He shouts "nevers" at his father, when the father wants to remind him of "always." Take a look at verse 29. The older brother says, "Look, these many years I have served you, and I have *never* disobeyed your command, yet you *never* gave me a young goat." Never! Some of us are like this with God. We raise our fists and shout: "You never! I have never done anything wrong. I have never been unfaithful, and you have never given me anything. You have never given me the health, the job, the family, and the success that I wanted. You never do anything for me." But do you see how the father replies with "always"? In verse 31, he says, "Son, you are *always* with me, and all that is mine is yours." We thumb our nose at God and say that we've never done anything wrong and that he never does anything for us. And God comes back to us and says, "You are always with me."

The parable is about God's love for two lost sons. We must not overlook either kind of sinner.

Some of us don't like prodigals. They're messy. They're dirty. They're spiritual wrecks. And some of us are just the opposite. We love to hear about prodigals being saved; it's the older brothers we can't stand. We love to take a good pharisaical squint at all the self-righteous Pharisees out there. We hate the holier-than-thou types, so proud and put together—which is why we must realize that God is eager to find all kinds of sinners. He runs to the prodigal and embraces him. The father welcomes the younger son home and forgives his sins. But then he also invites the older son to come inside (v. 28) and entreats him tenderly: "Son, you are always with me, and all that is mine is yours." The father is eager to lavish his love on both sons, provided the prodigal heads home and the proud one is able to receive the rest of his family.[3]

---

[3] The difference in language between verses 30 and 32 is instructive. The older brother calls the prodigal "this son of yours," while the father refers to him as "your brother." The sin of the Pharisees was in refusing to see the family of God as God the Father sees it.

Are we prepared to seek and to find all kinds of sinners? Are we willing to plead with both younger brothers and older brothers, and have both of them in the same church? Jesus leaves the parable open-ended on purpose. He doesn't tell us what the other brother does. We don't know whether he goes back in the house with the prodigal or harrumphs his way to hell. Jesus refuses to tie up the loose ends because he means the parable to be an open invitation to the scribes and the Pharisees to repent. He's telling them it's not too late to adopt the father's attitude, to forgive the wayward, and to join in on the celebration. It's not too late to see that the family of God is a place for all kinds of lost people—including those they hate, and even including themselves.

Third, *let us be marked in our lives and in our churches by the experience and the expectation of joy.* The kingdom is not present where the experience of joy is absent. Yes, there are seasons of lamentation, great struggle, and questioning in the Christian life. The Psalms give us all sorts of language for that. But if there is no evidence of joy in your life and in your church, you ought to wonder if the kingdom has truly come. The sharp contrast in Luke 15 is between the disdain of the Pharisees and the celebration of heaven. God's people are always marked by the *experience* of joy.

And they are marked by the *expectation* of joy. If we understand the gospel and the sort of God we worship, how can we be anything but hopeful people? Do you believe that God is seeking the lost? Do you believe he can find what he is looking for? This is the good news of believing in the sovereignty of God: our God seeks and he finds. Do you believe that?

Maybe you've been discouraged, wondering if you're just wasting your time as a Christian, feeling like nothing interesting will ever happen in your home or in your church. Maybe you've lost any expectation of joy. There's a scene in *The Incredibles* where Mr. Incredible, a superhero in disguise, picks up a car and is about to slam it to the ground. Suddenly, he notices a little boy on his tricycle in the driveway who can't believe what he's seeing. He's absolutely amazed. Later in the movie, the same kid is in the driveway again, just watching for Mr. Incredible to show his power. A little annoyed, the superhero asks the boy, "Well, what are you waiting for?" The boy says: "I don't know. Something amazing, I guess." Are you waiting for something amazing from God? We all should be. He seeks. He finds. He rejoices. He restores to us the joy of our salvation.

Have you long since lost the joy of your salvation? Has it been a while since anything in the Christian life felt like celebration to you? Have you forgotten how pleased God is with the prodigal who repents? And do you know how happy he is with the humble and faithful who never leave? Can you believe it, little sheep—you've been brought back to the fold? Can you believe it, little coin—you've been put back in your place? Can you believe it, lost sons and daughters—you have a home with the Father?

The sheep can recognize the voice of their master. Don't close your ears if you hear the Good Shepherd speaking to you. Joy awaits on the other side of repentance—for all kinds of sinners. Heaven is on alert for another ticker-tape parade. But it's only for those who are sick enough to be healed, weak enough to be saved, lost enough to be found.

6

JESUS AND MONEY

Luke 16:1–15

Stephen Um

The parable found in Luke 16:1–15 has been called "one of the strangest stories that Jesus tells."[1] As one scholar put it, "no other parable has caused as much perplexity and has received as many interpretations as this one."[2] Needless to say, one must approach such a text with a measure of hermeneutical humility, knowing that numerous orthodox, evangelical interpreters have differed in their understanding of the pericope. Though the main point of the passage seems clear, many have differed on the interpretive nuances. The result of this hermeneutical haze is that we rarely hear sermons or read reflections on what has been called the parable of the "dishonest manager." This narrative, it has been said, "takes the prize for being most ignored."[3] However, as we will see, the passage is filled with important insight and perspective, particularly as it relates to our given topic: Jesus and money.

It is no secret that Jesus talked a lot about money. In fact, he

---

[1] D. A. Carson, *For the Love of God: A Daily Companion for Discovering the Riches of God's Word,* vol. 1 (Wheaton, IL: Crossway, 2006), March 2.
[2] R. C. H. Lenski, *The Interpretation of St. Luke's Gospel 12–24* (Minneapolis: Augsburg Fortress, 2008), 830.
[3] Eugene H. Peterson, *Tell It Slant: A Conversation on the Language of Jesus in His Stories and Prayers* (Grand Rapids: Eerdmans, 2008), 99.

"warns people far more often about greed than about sex."[4] While Jesus did clearly speak against sexual sin, he spent more time on the subject of money because of the insidious nature of greed. Here is a litmus test: when was the last time you pounded your chest in repentance and said, "Lord, spare me from my greed!" I would venture to say that you have not done this recently. For one reason or another, we tend to assume that this is an area of temptation and sin with which we do not struggle or which we have simply overcome. This is precisely why Jesus goes out of his way to say, "Take care, and be on your guard against all covetousness" (Luke 12:15). The point is this: greed is insidious. We must recognize the seductive power of greed, and we must not assume that we are unaffected by it.

However, while it is important to recognize the subtlety of greed, it is equally important to disinfect our view of money. For many, *money* itself has become a dirty word. The broader culture's perspective on money is troublesome, and the misuses and abuses of money are simply too glaring. But while money has certainly been twisted, we must understand that at its core it is a good gift from God intended to be used for his purposes. As a "means of exchange," a currency, it is "no more inherently evil than any other material thing God created."[5] Sondra Wheeler helps us get a sense for this:

> There is in the New Testament no pure asceticism that depreciates material reality as intrinsically evil. . . . The dangers of distraction and entanglement, of misplaced trust and loyalty that inhere in ownership are all brought forward, but there is no repudiation of material goods as such. . . . The necessity and goodness of wealth as a resource for the meeting of human needs are affirmed . . . the same epistles which condemn greed

---

[4] Timothy Keller, *Counterfeit Gods: The Empty Promises of Money, Sex, and Power, and the Only Hope That Matters* (New York: Dutton, 2009), 53. Keller's chapter on money in *Counterfeit Gods*, along with his unpublished sermons on the topic, have influenced my thinking on the subject.

[5] Ben Witherington III, *Jesus and Money: A Guide for Times of Financial Crisis* (Grand Rapids: Brazos, 2012), 167.

as idolatrous can commend provision for oneself and one's family as a duty.[6]

In short, money is a gift from God, and greed is an insidious spoiler of that gift. How then can money be restored to its gift status? And how can we be transformed from greedy hoarders to generous stewards? To answer these questions, we first need to look more closely at the difficulties we have with money.

The Problem of Money

In the parable of the dishonest manager, Jesus tells his disciples a story about a very rich man who has entrusted the care of his possessions to a manager. The rich man is told that his manager has been mismanaging and wasting the possessions that are in his care. "So he called him in and asked him, 'What is this I hear about you? Give an account of your management, because you cannot be manager any longer'" (Luke 16:2 NIV). The man has wasted and squandered his employer's possessions (16:1; cf. 15:13), and as a result, he is going to be fired. The cost of this dismissal will be the loss not only of income, but also of an enjoyable vocation that affords him enviable social status.[7] Needless to say, the dishonest manager is backed into a corner, and it is through his less-than-ideal circumstances that we see the potential dangers of money.

The first moment of tension in the story comes as we await the manager's response to his rich employer. How will he react to the accusation of mismanagement? In the previous chapter of Luke, we saw a beautiful picture of a prodigal son coming to his senses. The son realizes that he will have to look outside of himself for his salvation, and he casts himself upon the mercy of his father (15:11–24). We find the opposite happening here. Rather than admitting his wrongdoing and then repenting, the dishonest manager hunkers down in his self-sufficient obstinacy. He does not even respond

---

[6] Sondra Ely Wheeler, *Wealth as Peril and Obligation: The New Testament on Possessions* (Grand Rapids: Eerdmans, 1995), 133–34, as quoted in Witherington, *Jesus and Money*, 143.

[7] Joel B. Green, *The Gospel of Luke*, New International Commentary on the New Testament (Grand Rapids: Eerdmans, 1997), 590.

to his employer; instead, "the manager said to himself . . ." (v. 3). While the prodigal son turns outward for help, the manager turns inward. While the prodigal pleads for mercy, the manager doubles down on his scheme and refuses to admit his need for mercy. Here are two radically different heart postures.

What drives him to respond in this manner? The dishonest manager shows us how the human heart can idolatrously twist money in three ways.

Money Can Become Your Security

In Luke 16:3, we find an individual who is insecure, nervous, anxious, and afraid: "And the manager said to himself, 'What shall I do, since my master is taking the management away from me? I am not strong enough to dig, and I am ashamed to beg.'" The manager's security is entirely wrapped up with his work and the money it affords him. The threat of his position being stripped away from him is tantamount to losing his life. He is sinking into despair.

The passage proceeds to give us a picture of the manager working out his solution—his attempt to hold onto his self-derived security. But rather than looking away from the problem for assistance, he goes back to the problem itself in hopes of finding help. Undue trust in money is the problem, but rather than recognizing that problem, he continues to place his trust in financial resources as a way to purchase his security. Here is the manager's revealing reasoning:

> "I have decided what to do, so that when I am removed from management, people may receive me into their houses." So, summoning his master's debtors one by one, he said to the first, "How much do you owe my master?" He said, "A hundred measures of oil." He said to him, "Take your bill, and sit down quickly and write fifty." Then he said to another, "And how much do you owe?" He said, "A hundred measures of wheat." He said to him, "Take your bill, and write eighty." (Luke 16:4–7)

The manager is seeking to make himself the benefactor of his employer's customers by showing them generosity at his employer's expense. His hope is that they will reciprocate his apparent kindness later by showing him hospitality and welcoming him into their homes.[8] Rather than dealing with the issue between himself and his master, the manager is entirely focused on securing his future. He knows that he has been sacked. He knows that his job is lost forever. But although the security of his past is irretrievable, he hopes that he might purchase some security for his future—at least a roof over his head—through his mock generosity. The gift of money has been idolatrously twisted into a faulty means of procuring temporary security.

How do you know if something has become your functional security? Simply ask what would happen if it were removed from your life. How would you respond if your money, assets, or career were taken away from you? Would your life lose all meaning? Would you fall into insecurity, anxiety, or despair? Perhaps you would respond like the dishonest manager responds in this passage. He does everything in his power to secure his future because to lose his resources and relationships is to lose everything that gives him a sense of security and purpose.

David Powlison has suggested that in order to identify the functional securities in our lives, it is important to ask "X-ray questions"—pointed questions that help us to get past the surface level and into the motivating engine of the heart.[9] If it is true that greed is subtle and insidious, then we may have to look beneath the surface to see if it is at work in our lives. I've adapted some of his questions here:

- Where do you bank your hopes? On your ability to earn, save, and multiply money?
- What do you fear? Economic downturn, failed investments, job loss, financial collapse?

---

[8] Ibid., 593.
[9] For a full list of Powlison's X-ray questions, see the seventh chapter of *Seeing with New Eyes: Counseling and the Human Condition through the Lens of Scripture* (Phillipsburg, NJ: P&R, 2003).

- Where do you find refuge, safety, comfort, and security? In assets, possessions, savings, tenure, or a retirement plan?

The point of these questions is not to say that sound investments and retirement planning are wrong. The Bible doesn't speak against investments and wise planning per se, but it does speak against *bad* investments and *self-interested* planning. In the parable of the talents (Matt. 25:14–30), Jesus tells a story to demonstrate that God wants us to increase the assets that have been entrusted to us. To this end, we should seek to steward the resources we have been given wisely. We must ask ourselves: "Am I investing well to increase the Master's assets because my treasure is in heaven?[10] Or am I investing poorly because my treasure is here on earth?"

The end result of unwise, self-interested investments is not simply mismanagement of God's resources, but robbery of God himself. If God is the Creator, Ruler, and owner of everything, then our failure to carry out our obligations as stewards of the Master's assets is to rob him of that which is rightfully (and actually) his. When you gain your sense of security from money, you fail to properly steward the resources that God has entrusted to you, and you steal from the hand that has graciously provided for you. Remember: we are not owners; we are stewards.[11]

Money Can Become Your Master

No servant can serve two masters, for either he will hate the one and love the other, or he will be devoted to the one and despise the other. You cannot serve God and money. (Luke 16:13)

Jesus makes it very clear that the result of finding your security in money is ultimately enslavement to money. The manager has the opportunity to turn, repent, and patch things up with his master,

---

[10] I am indebted to Don Carson for the language of increasing or "improving the Master's assets." See D. A. Carson, "How Should We Wait for Jesus?" *Decision Magazine*, May 2009.

[11] I am grateful to my friend Michael Keller for his suggestion that stewardship can be placed along the one-story plotline of the Bible. His insights were invaluable in the development of this sermon. We have looked at creation here. We will develop the perspectives on the fall and redemption below.

but he does not even consider this because he is actually serving another master, namely, money. This can easily happen to us. Rather than possessing money as a means of exchange—as a currency to be invested for the Master's purposes—we can be possessed by money. Rather than controlling money, we can be controlled by money. Rather than managing money, we find ourselves managed by money.

This is precisely what had happened to the rich young ruler (Luke 18). Though he thinks that he has kept the Ten Commandments since his youth, in reality he has not kept even the first commandment. When Jesus instructs him to sell all that he has and distribute it to the poor, he balks (vv. 22–24). God had instructed, "You shall have no other gods before me" (Ex. 20:3), but the rich young ruler has been mastered by a different god. He is enslaved by money—a master to which he is obedient, even over and above God himself.

Has money mastered you? Consider these X-ray questions:[12]

- What do you think about the most? About money that you have earned or plan to earn? About the balance in your bank account? About the status of your investments?
- What do you fantasize about? About the way your life would look if you had more money? About things you would like to own or places you would like to go?
- What are your thought patterns? How often do you think about money? Do you measure your self-worth against your statement balances or investments? Do you measure others by the amount of wealth you perceive them to have?
- What are your priorities? Do you make many or most decisions based upon money? Is money the driving motivation for your work? Are you able to give your money away freely, or do you find it difficult to live with an open hand?

Many Christians are unwittingly enslaved by money, consistently thinking, "If I only had this, then I might be able to get

---

[12] See note 9.

this." If this is your thought pattern—if your fantasy life revolves around getting, owning, and enjoying the things that money can buy—then money may be your master.

This is not an uncommon experience. Because of the fall, it is not unusual for humans to be controlled by money. As a result, we are stingy and selfish when it comes to our financial resources. But here's the problem: stinginess is not simply a neutral or temperamental disposition. Stinginess is evidence that money has power over us—that we live in slavery to sin. Rather than being gracious stewards of the money God has given us, we are enslaved hoarders of resources that are not really ours.

Money Can Become Your Lover

You know you are in love with something if, when someone attacks it, you grow defensive. That is exactly what happens to the Pharisees who are listening in on Jesus's parable: "The Pharisees, who were lovers of money, heard all these things, and they ridiculed him. And he said to them, 'You are those who justify yourselves before men, but God knows your hearts. For what is exalted among men is an abomination in the sight of God'" (Luke 16:14–15). "Lovers of money" is not a title that many of us would like to be assigned, but the Pharisees earn it with their sneering, snorting response to Jesus's parable.[13] Money has a grip on their hearts; they react to Jesus as if their lover has been spurned.

So we see that not only is it possible to be enslaved by money, but that it is possible to be in love with the very thing that is enslaving you. And just like other lovers, money demands your fidelity; it wants to have a faithful, monogamous relationship with you. You can't love money and love something else. Devotion to money will lead you to despise everything that threatens it (v. 13).

In his classic book *The Denial of Death*, Ernest Becker introduces the idea of apocalyptic romance or "the romantic love

---

[13] The Greek behind 16:14's "ridiculed" "literally means 'to turn one's nose up' at someone; it indicates strong contempt." Darrell L. Bock, *Luke 9:51–24:53,* Baker Exegetical Commentary on the New Testament (Grand Rapids: Baker Academic, 2008), 1349.

'cosmology of two.'"[14] In essence, he claims that if a love relationship becomes your ultimate good—even if it is good in and
of itself—it will become apocalyptic in nature. The end of the
relationship will be interpreted as the end of the world.[15] This is
precisely what has happened to the dishonest manager. He can't
imagine his life apart from the security that he has obtained by
way of his financial misdealings. He has treasured and loved his
money above all else, and it has gained an apocalyptic significance
for him. Now his world is coming apart at the seams. As one
commentator puts it, "It is the love of wealth, not the amount of
wealth that starves the soul."[16] The dishonest manager is starving
his soul to death.

Let's think in relation to the Bible's one-story plotline. In light
of God's creation and ownership of our world, if we act like owners
instead of stewards, we are guilty not simply of mismanagement
but of robbery.[17] In light of man's fall into sin, to be tight-fisted
is not simply stinginess but slavery. And now, in light of Christ's
redemptive work and the subsequent call to steward our resources,
when we eschew generosity, we not only fail to perform our duty
but commit adultery. A lack of generosity is proof that some other
lover has captured our affections.

The potential problems we encounter with money are enormous. So what hope can there be? How can we ensure that money
does not become our security, our master, or our lover? To answer
these questions, we need to explore the gospel and its power to free
us from our insidious idolization of money.

---

[14] Ernest Becker, *The Denial of Death* (New York: The Free Press, 1973), 165. Tim Keller also cites Becker's
understanding of "apocalyptic romance" in *Counterfeit Gods*, 28.

[15] Ibid. "How can a human being be a god-like 'everything' to another? No human relationship can bear the
burden of godhood, and the attempt has to take its toll in some way on both parties" (166). "After all, what
is it that we want when we elevate the love partner to the position of God? We want redemption—nothing
less. We want to be rid of our faults, of our feeling of nothingness. We want to be justified, to know that our
creation has not been in vain. We turn to the love partner for the experience of the heroic, for perfect valida-
tion; we expect them to 'make us good' through love. Needless to say, human partners can't do this" (167).

[16] Arthur Simon, *How Much Is Enough? Hungering for God in an Affluent Culture* (Grand Rapids: Baker, 2004),
17. Original emphasis removed.

[17] The word for "wasting" in 16:1 is last used in 15:13 to refer to the way that the younger prodigal "squandered" his inheritance through "reckless living." The dishonest manager did not simply have a competency
issue (i.e., he was a poor manager), but a character issue (i.e., he was a reckless manager).

The Power to Free Us from the Grip of Money

Security in Christ

One of the more difficult and enigmatic portions of our text is verse 8, where we read: "The master commended the dishonest manager for his shrewdness. For the sons of this world are more shrewd in dealing with their own generation than the sons of light." This verse has confounded commentators over the ages. After all we have learned about the dishonest manager's problem with money, it is normal to wonder how he receives commendation from his master. But look very carefully. Jesus does not say that this man is commended for his unrighteousness and dishonesty. He is commended for a very particular portion of his behavior, namely, his shrewdness.

Don Carson helps us cut through this potentially confusing portion of our text: "It cannot mean that Jesus advocates unscrupulous business practices. The point is that the manager used resources under his control (though not properly his) to prepare for his own future."[18] David Wenham reaches a similar conclusion: "This parable is not a commendation of dishonest stewardship, but of shrewd forethought and preparation for a future crisis. The application of the parable in Luke 16:8 is unambiguous in this respect."[19] This is the point Jesus is making: if the children of this world are willing to plan for their future and they manage assets with that in mind, how much more should we, as children of God, manage the Master's assets with the future in mind (v. 9)?

Here is the essential difference: children of this world ruthlessly manage their resources to secure their future; children of God graciously manage their resources because their future is already secure. Those who are in Christ have an "already" experience of their future inheritance (Eph. 1:11, 14). They live with the full security of a "living hope" (1 Pet. 1:3). When you realize that the riches of God's grace in Christ are already yours, you can cease

---

[18] Carson, *For the Love of God,* vol. 1, March 2.

[19] David Wenham, *The Parables of Jesus* (Downers Grove, IL: InterVarsity, 1989), 164.

trying to secure your future by means of financial management (or mismanagement). Whether you are rich or poor, your future is secure. When you fully grasp this, you are free to manage your God-given resources in an other-focused way.

Mastered by Christ

As we have seen, part of the difficulty with properly stewarding our resources is that we are easily enslaved by money. Rather than controlling and using money to increase the Master's assets, we find ourselves controlled and used by money itself. When this is the case, Jesus's teaching that "no servant can serve two masters" (Luke 16:13) ceases to be encouraging and starts to sound impossible. God rightly demands that we be exclusively devoted to him, but we find proof in our own lives (anxiety, workaholism, etc.) that we are actually attempting to serve two masters. So how can those who are enslaved by money—unfaithful servants—be set free to serve God with a singular devotion? How can we who stumble and waver meet the high demands of God's law?

In a very real sense, we are unable to meet the demand for a singular devotion, and so we must either receive the punishment for our dual-heartedness, or find one who is able to meet the demand in our place. In short, we need to be mastered by an authority of grace that expresses itself through a mastery of service. We need to be mastered by a faithful servant who will meet the high demands of the law in our place, and who will willingly receive the punishment for our dishonest management.

God demands perfect service, and that service is perfectly fulfilled in the person of Jesus Christ. Likewise, God demands satisfaction for wrongdoing, and that satisfaction is perfectly provided by Jesus in his work on the cross. As the perfect, singularly devoted suffering servant, he has done that which was out of our reach. And as our perfect, singularly devoted Master, he has made us his own, setting us free from slavery to all other competing masters. As a result, we are now free to steward our resources generously as a declaration of our singular devotion to him—our faithful, suffering servant-Master.[20]

Loved by Christ

But how can our hearts be won over by Christ so that our motivations and desires actually begin to shift? Our hearts have to be dealt with and transformed by God. And how does this happen? Look at Jesus's interaction with the Pharisees in Luke 16:15: "He said to them, 'You are those who justify yourselves before men, but God knows your hearts. For what is exalted among men is an abomination in the sight of God.'"

Like the Pharisees, we are consistently pulled by the love of this world—seeking to prove our worth before others but paying little attention to what is actually happening in our hearts. We see this dynamic at play in Luke 18, where Jesus tells the parable of the Pharisee and the tax collector (vv. 9–14). While the Pharisee is concerned primarily with his appearance and what will justify him in the eyes of men, the tax collector is concerned to deal with God on a heart level regardless of what it may look like to others. Jesus says: "The tax collector, standing far off, would not even lift up his eyes to heaven, but beat his breast, saying, 'God, be merciful to me, a sinner!' I tell you, this man went down to his house justified, rather than the other. For everyone who exalts himself will be humbled, but the one who humbles himself will be exalted" (vv. 13–14).

---

[20] Though Luke does not make an explicit connection with Isaiah's messianic suffering servant, the biblical-theological theme of "servant" pushes us to resolve the tension by finding its resolution in Christ. When we read Luke carefully, we actually find reason to make this connection to Christ as the perfectly faithful servant.

In the Old Testament, Israel was called to worship and serve God alone (Deut. 6:13; cf. Luke 1:54). The language of "servant" would later be applied to David (2 Sam. 7:5, 8, 26; Luke 1:69). While Israel and David failed to perform this task, Jesus—the true Israel, the greater David (Luke 1:32)—came to perfectly fulfill this worship and service (Luke 4:8). For this purpose, the Spirit came upon him at his baptism: "The Spirit of the Lord is upon me, because he has anointed me to proclaim good news to the poor. He has sent me to proclaim liberty to the captives and recovering of sight to the blind, to set at liberty those who are oppressed, to proclaim the year of the Lord's favor" (Luke 4:18–19). This, of course, is a reference to Isaiah 61, which many scholars regard as the fifth "servant song" in Isaiah because of its linguistic connection to the first servant song in chapter 42: "Behold my servant, whom I uphold, my chosen, in whom my soul delights; I have put my Spirit upon him; he will bring forth justice to the nations" (42:1). It is ultimately this "servant" who will "make many to be accounted righteous, and he shall bear their iniquities" (53:11). In this way, Jesus Christ fulfills the role of the suffering servant through his perfect service and bearing of punishment. It is in this context that we must hear Jesus's statement: "But I am among you as the one who serves" (Luke 22:27).

The Pharisees were all about self-justification. They sought salvation in their efforts to appear righteous before men, and they loved money to the extent that it enabled them to achieve this end. The tax collector knew that his appearance before men held no real weight and that his money had no purchase in God's economy. The only means of justification was to expose his heart and throw himself upon the mercy of God. This is exactly what we are called to do, and when God does this justifying work in our hearts, it is radically transformative.

Many years ago, when I was pursuing doctoral studies in the United Kingdom, my eldest daughter, who was about six at the time, participated in a "sports day" at her school. The purpose was to give the kids a chance to compete individually and collectively. On that day, whenever a child would win an event, he or she would receive a coveted "trophy sticker." Now, I realize that a trophy sticker does not hold all that much significance for adults, but for a six-year-old, it means a lot.

As it happened, after about thirty minutes, my daughter was the only one who didn't have a trophy sticker. While I was concerned, I was sure that if we gave it another thirty minutes, she would earn one, or at least bump into someone and accidentally pick one up on her shoulder. But after two hours, she came off the field with no trophy sticker. Her head was down. We got into the car. We drove a couple of miles to our home. When we arrived, she went into her room and slammed the door.

What was I supposed to do? As her father, I wanted to care for her. So I went into her room, where she was crying. I said: "Honey, it's okay. I'm so proud of you. You did great. You participated, you ran, and you were great. Your sister thinks you're great, your mom thinks you're great, and I think you're great."

Then she rebutted: "I don't care if you think I was great, Dad. I didn't get a trophy sticker."

What made the conversation even harder was her next move. She said: "Daddy, do you know why I wasn't running very fast today? It was because of my trainers!"

I said, "Excuse me?"

And she said, "You bought me cheap sneakers!"

As a father, my heart was grieved for two reasons. First, I *had* bought her cheap sneakers. I was a poor doctoral student! But second, I was grieved because my six-year-old daughter desperately wanted to be accepted. How was I supposed to respond? I could have said: "It's okay. You'll do better next time. I'll buy you a pair of Nikes." That would have been false comfort. Or I could have said, "You need to train harder in order to be more competitive next time!" That would have crushed her in the event that she wasn't able to compete at that level. Instead, I told her about the story of grace. I told her that it is not about how you appear or how much you achieve. It is not about how much faster you can run than others. It is not about justifying yourself in the eyes of others with sneakers and trophy stickers.

Ultimately, we must realize the difference between the judgment of this world and the judgment of God. The world accepts us when we are at our best, but it rejects us when we are at our worst. Only God rejects our best efforts at self-justification *and* freely and fully accepts us at our worst. "He who did not spare his own Son but gave him up for us all, how will he not also with him graciously give us all things?" (Rom. 8:32). Only this kind of love can transform us at the heart level, leading us to recognize that all that we call our own is actually a gracious gift from God, and stirring our hearts to reflect and engender the self-donating love that has been so freely given to us.

What, then, does this look like when it begins to be worked out in our lives?

The Use of Money: Implications for Gospel-Shaped Stewardship[21]

First, God's ownership of everything means that we are not actually owners but simply stewards. In other words, we are *obligated* to be

---

[21] Michael Keller's insights were particularly helpful in framing this section. See note 11.

generous stewards. Because our future is secure in Christ, we are now able to view ourselves as completely free from our insecurities and anxieties. We are not shareholders with something to lose but stockbrokers with everything to gain for our Master! We must realize that we are simply investing someone else's resources. If this is true, we really have nothing to lose, and knowing that gives us the freedom to be radically generous.

Second, the fall's effect on our approach to money means that our freedom is on the line; money can potentially enslave us. This means that we *need* to be generous stewards in order to demonstrate our freedom from the grip of money consistently. Every time we give of our time and resources, we are telling ourselves that money is not the functional slavemaster of our heart. Ultimately, Jesus's perfect service on our behalf means that we are objectively free from the power of sin and free to take up our role as stewards.

Third, the redemption that God has provided for us in Christ means that our fidelity is on the line. Money can potentially seduce us. However, when the reality that Christ has purchased us for himself explodes in our hearts, we no longer give because we are obligated to give or because we need to give, but because we *want* to give. Truly knowing that Christ has given himself for us creates in us the desire to give ourselves and all that we have to him. When Christ is our treasure, we can invest freely in the things that bring him joy.

Finally, we must allow the gospel of God's grace to be our constant and solitary motivation for generous giving. Consider Paul's gospel-shaped logic in 2 Corinthians 8. Here is the context: there is an economically distressed church in Jerusalem, and he is appealing to all of the other churches to pick up the slack. He had appealed to the Corinthians in chapter 15 of his first letter to them, but they have not yet responded. Other churches, such as the one in Macedonia, are eager to give despite their own economic hardships, but the Corinthians have been slow to follow through.

We might expect Paul to get tough with them—to draw heavily on his apostolic authority and pressure these stingy Christians to give what they have pledged. And he would be well within his rights to do so. But he takes another route. Observe his appeal to the grace of God as a motivation for generous giving: "I say this not as a command, but to prove by the earnestness of others that your love also is genuine. For you know the grace of our Lord Jesus Christ, that though he was rich, yet for your sake he became poor, so that you by his poverty might become rich" (2 Cor. 8:8–9).

The perfect servant who had everything—the One who served, trusted, and loved his Master perfectly—came and gave his life to save stingy, insecure, enslaved, adulterous, dishonest managers. He did not come to shoulder part of our burden and alleviate a portion of our debt. He came to shoulder the entire burden and to cancel all of the debt at the cost of his life. He who was rich became poor so that we by his poverty might become rich. And his gracious act of self-giving transforms and reorders our affections so that we are not simply *obligated* to give and do not simply *need* to give, but ultimately and joyfully *desire* to give in grateful response to his lavish grace.

7

JESUS BETRAYED AND CRUCIFIED

Luke 22:39–23:49

Gary Millar

If you have ever flown into Ireland, one thing surely struck you: Ireland is remarkably green. What the tourist board is not so quick to point out is the rather obvious cause of this: it rains all the time. I can sum up almost forty-five years spent in Ireland with one word: *damp*. Or perhaps three better words: *cold and damp*.

Then, in the providence of God, we were uprooted and taken to Queensland, Australia, where the tourist slogan is, "Beautiful one day, perfect the next." Every day, I get out of bed and thank God for the sunshine. I say, "Where have you been all my life?" Sometimes friends ask, "How do you cope with the heat?" I just say, "I love it." I've got forty-five years of stored-up thankfulness to draw on. It will be a long time before I ever take the weather in Brisbane for granted.

But taking people for granted—well, that's a different matter. Taking people for granted is easy to do—in fact, most of us can pull it off without even thinking about it—but it is never a good idea. In marriage, it causes hurt and tension. In families, it can cause long-term fallout. In the workplace, it is one sure way of ensuring a high staff turnover. In church, it contributes to bitterness and burnout, making people feel used. Taking each other for granted is not a good thing. It's generally a recipe for simmering resentment.

But the consequences of taking each other for granted are nothing compared to the toxic effect on our relationship with God of taking the Lord Jesus Christ for granted.

Even among committed evangelicals—even among those who might read the plenary addresses from The Gospel Coalition's National Conference!—it is possible that many take the Lord Jesus for granted. Many are passionate about understanding and teaching the gospel. But are we passionate about Christ himself? To quote Paul Tripp: "Are we more drawn to ideas than Jesus? Are we more drawn to ministry success than personal growth? Are we more excited by the next phase of the strategic plan than the glory of God and the grandeur of his grace?"[1] The truth is that we are all more than capable of taking Jesus for granted.

We may love theology, we may love strategizing, we may love reading, we may love discussing, we may love exegesis, we may love preaching, we may love dreaming and encouraging—but the prior question to all this is: Do we love Jesus Christ? Are we constantly bowled over by his tenderness and his steely resolve, his incisive wit, his flawless insight, his delightful playfulness, his vibrant personality, his overwhelming personal attractiveness, his sheer God-embodying beauty? If not, then we need to read the Gospels, because the Gospels give us a person. Of course, the Gospels are dripping with theology. But the theology is embodied. It's incarnated. In the Gospels, and in Luke in particular, theology comes not so much in creedal summary statements, but in the flesh in the person of Jesus. We must not miss Jesus.

A simple reading of the five hundred words of Luke 22:39–23:49 instantly creates an impression of Jesus Christ as the one who keeps his head when everyone around him is losing theirs. For several reasons, Jesus stands out.

---

[1] Paul David Tripp, *Dangerous Calling: Confronting the Unique Challenges of Pastoral Ministry* (Wheaton, IL: Crossway, 2012), 120.

Jesus Stands Out Because He Is in Control

First, he stands out because he is in control—as a look through the narrative clearly reveals. He leads the way to the Mount of Olives (Luke 22:39). It's Jesus who prays and tells his friends to pray (vv. 40–41). When they are falling apart, overcome with grief, he stays disciplined and focused (v. 45). Jesus takes the initiative with Judas (v. 48). He ensures that the disciples' resistance stops as soon as it starts (v. 51). Jesus says to the chief priests and officers of the temple and elders, "But this is your hour, and the power of darkness" (v. 53). Jesus is not taken; he hands himself over. He is in complete control. This is not just submission to fate. This is not just embracing the inevitable. Jesus is taking all the initiative. He is making things happen.

The contrast between Jesus and Peter could hardly be more stark as Peter follows Jesus into the high priest's courtyard (22:54–62). Whereas Jesus is measured, Peter is panicky. Whereas Jesus speaks calmly, Peter blurts out lies.

When Jesus comes face to face with the chief priests (22:66–71), he not only refuses to be bullied by them, but he obliquely reminds them of his authority as the Son of Man, the One who will ultimately judge them: "If I tell you, you will not believe, and if I ask you, you will not answer. But from now on the Son of Man shall be seated at the right hand of the power of God" (vv. 67–69). There is a mind-blowing sense in all this that the One who is on trial is actually orchestrating the trial.

Luke portrays Jesus's refusal to engage with Pilate also as a calm and considered strategy. In the face of ongoing injustice, Jesus himself directs the outcome! His silence (23:9) is not despair or stubbornness. He stays silent in order to move things forward toward his ultimate goal. Jesus hasn't given up. He knows exactly what he is doing.

Pilate seems confused. He tries to pass the buck to Herod and to the crowd (23:7). The religious leaders try to shout and scream in an effort to control the event (v. 10). But the prisoner? He is unflinching and resolute. He won't put on a show for Herod (v. 9). He won't be drawn into defending himself in a sham trial. He is silent. And by his controlled silence, he brings his death for us one step closer. By choosing not to speak, he exercises perfect control of the situation.

If we need confirmation that Jesus isn't simply in despair or being swept along helplessly by events, Luke provides it for us (23:26–31). When Jesus does speak, it's obvious he is holding it together; his mind is fixed firmly on what he has come to do and on how it will affect ordinary people—like the women who are so upset to see this man walking to his execution: "And there followed him a great multitude of the people and of women who were mourning and lamenting for him. But turning to them Jesus said, 'Daughters of Jerusalem, do not weep for me, but weep for yourselves and for your children'" (vv. 27–28). Even as he walks to his death, he is concerned for other people. He is thinking about the judgment to come, both the interim judgment on Jerusalem and ultimately the final judgment beyond that (vv. 29–31).

Even when we reach the cross and Jesus is hoisted between the two criminals, ironically, he has never been more in control (23:32–49). As he dies to save, he is mocked for his inability to save (vv. 35–37). But when he himself speaks, what does he say? "Father forgive them, they know not what they do" (v. 34) and "Today you will be with me in paradise" (v. 43). This man is in control. He is even in control of the eternal destiny of those around him. This man has the power to forgive. This is the Judge of all the earth, who is in total control of all events.

It's almost the end of overtime. It's time for one last play. Whom do you want to have the ball? You want the calmest guy you have out there. Imagine that the security of the nation is at risk, threat levels have gone through the roof, and attack is imminent. Whom do you want to have the nuclear codes? Whom do you want making the final call on what to do or not to do? You want a guy who's calm under pressure. Imagine you are diagnosed with a malignant, fast-growing tumor, and are rushed to a hospital for immediate surgery.

Whom do you want to perform the operation? I want a guy who is calm; someone whose hand doesn't shake; someone who can cope with pressure; someone who is in complete control.

That's how Luke presents Jesus in these chapters. He is under extreme pressure, pressure that we will never fathom. He is actually sweating drops of blood—and whether that's a metaphor or a medical condition, it is an indication of great stress. And yet, at every stage, Jesus is calm. He is in control of himself. But that's not all—and this is where Jesus leaves every sports star, every politician, and every surgeon far behind. It's not just that Jesus is in control of himself; he is in control of events themselves. It's not just that he is able to handle his own adrenaline; he is able to dictate the result. Jesus isn't able just to act wisely under pressure; he is able to determine the outcome. It's not just that he is able to respond skillfully to what he finds; he knows what he will find and has already mapped out the permanent solution to the deepest human problem of all. Jesus stands out in this narrative because he is in control of the entire sweep of human history even as he goes to his death.

At one level, yes, we must see someone who is "like a lamb that is led to the slaughter" (Isa. 53:7). But Isaiah also says, "Behold, my servant shall act wisely" (52:13). Yes, Jesus Christ is a victim—but the truth in this narrative is so much richer, deeper, and more moving than that, for the victim is utterly in control, moving powerfully and purposefully toward the completion of the mission he planned with his Father before the foundation of the world.

This is God's sovereignty in action. At this point in the Gospel, the sovereignty of God has a personal face.

Can you see how Jesus uses his control; how he exercises his power? He uses it for us. Instinctively, when you and I are given control of a situation, we use it to make life better for us and ours. We think and act selfishly. But not Jesus. This is the most powerful expression of determined selflessness the world has ever seen or will ever see. He uses his authority, exercises his control, and determines his destiny for the sake of you and me. Shouldn't that make us marvel at him?

When we say "Jesus Christ is Lord," we are saying that he is in control of the history of the world. And where do we see that most clearly? We see it as Jesus walks to his own death, as he uses his power and control not for himself but for people like us. Surely we cannot take this Jesus for granted.

Jesus Stands Out Because He Is Innocent

It is not just the fact that he is in control both of himself and of events that makes Jesus stand out. He also stands out because Luke is at great pains to show that Jesus is innocent. As he is interviewed by the high priest, and as he appears before the Sanhedrin, Pilate, Herod, and then Pilate again, Luke says over and over again that Jesus is completely without fault.

Back near the start of the passage (22:47–53), Luke contrasts Jesus's obvious innocence with the way in which he is treated by the authorities. Jesus is praying; they come with armed men. They draw their swords; Jesus heals an injured slave. Jesus speaks gently and respectfully, whereas they abuse and blaspheme him.

When the kangaroo court is convened (22:66–71), Jesus's innocence is obvious. But despite the lack of evidence, they rush him to Pilate in time for the daily court hearings. Pilate's verdict? "I find no guilt in this man" (23:4).

Herod echoes that verdict by implication (23:7–11). Herod questions Jesus at some length, but he doesn't answer. There is no new evidence. His innocence is just as obvious as it was before. Of course, that didn't stop the chief priests and the scribes from abusing him, and it doesn't stop Herod and his bodyguards from treating him with contempt, mocking him, dressing him up, and sending him back to Pilate. At this point, of course, he should be released. He is innocent. But he is hated, mocked, and humiliated.

Just so that we don't miss this, Luke records Pilate's own words: "You brought me this man as one who was misleading the people. And after examining him before you, behold, I did not find this man guilty of any of your charges against him. Neither did Herod, for he sent him back to us. Look, nothing deserving death has been done by him. I will therefore punish and release him" (23:14–16). Jesus is "officially" innocent, but the Jewish leaders keep pushing: "A third time [Pilate] said to them, 'Why, what evil has he done? I have found in him no guilt deserving death. I will therefore punish and release him'" (v. 22). Eventually, their voices prevail. Luke makes it very clear Pilate knows that he is condemning an innocent man.

Luke is less interested in Pilate's motivation—whether it is moral cowardice, political expediency, or both—and much more interested in establishing the fact beyond all doubt that Jesus is utterly innocent.

If you need even more proof of this, then just look at the closing verses of this long section. What's the verdict of the man dying next to Jesus? "We are receiving the due reward of our deeds; but this man has done nothing wrong" (23:41). Likewise, what is the verdict of the centurion commanding the death squad? "Certainly this man was innocent!" (v. 47). This is Luke's key point. All through these chapters, Jesus stands out because he is innocent. This is the most appalling miscarriage of justice in all human history.

Miscarriages of justice are always affecting. That's why movies such as *The Shawshank Redemption*, *In the Name of the Father*, *The Fugitive*, and a whole host of others are so powerful. But this is no mere miscarriage of justice. It's not just that Jesus is the wrong man. He is the perfect man. The righteous One. The pure One. He stands out from everyone else in this chapter; indeed, from everyone else who has ever walked on this planet. He is the perfect, innocent human being. And we killed him. He is the Son of Man, who is the Judge of all the earth. And we condemned him.

Place this man beside any of us and he stands out in blazing purity. The sweetest baby is exposed as a ball of snarling selfishness. The greatest humanitarian suddenly appears as a bundle of self-interest. Our grasping, self-serving, shameful black-heartedness serves only to illuminate his perfect innocence.

Aren't you so glad that he came? At last, here is a man we can count on; a man we can be proud of; a man we can look up to—a hero worth having. Here is a man in whom there is no pride, no lies, no trickery, no spin, no wishful thinking, and no dirty secrets, just innocence, holiness, and Godlikeness. He is a man so brimming with selfless love that he dies for us at the hands of people like us. The contrast between his innocence and our wickedness is so incredibly stark. It is so morally confronting. It's exposing. Really, how could we take this innocent God-man for granted?

Jesus Stands Out Because He Trusts God

Luke's account also highlights a third aspect of our Lord Jesus—as well as standing out as the innocent One who is in control, Jesus stands out as the One who trusts God in the face of the most horrific challenge ever faced by a human being.

Our passage is bracketed by two simple statements of Jesus that make clear that all he says and does is underwritten by straightforward trust in his Father. Yes, he is in control of his own emotions. Yes, at one level, he is the One pulling the strings. But we must not miss the fact that he also trusts his Father perfectly.

At the heart of his prayer in the garden are these words: "Father, if you are willing, remove this cup from me. Nevertheless, not my will, but yours, be done" (22:42). This unfathomable act of submission flows from a flawless trust in his Father. The same clear note is sounded at the end of Jesus's earthly life, as he prays with a loud voice, "Father, into your hands I commit my spirit!" (23:46). This is naked trust.

I suspect that this is why Luke chooses not to include every word that Jesus says during those long hours as his life ebbs away. He wants to make sure we get the fact that this innocent man, this man who remains in complete control even as those around him rage and conspire, is also the man who trusts God perfectly, flawlessly, unremittingly. Even as he faces the wrath of the Father, he trusts him. There is no other moment like this in all of history.

There is no one else like this. There is no one else worthy of our worship, our praise, and our trust.

And there is no one else who can trust for us. Have you ever thought about this? Our situation is so hopeless we actually need someone to trust God for us. One of the things I love about coming to the United States is seeing those four little words on coins and notes: "In God We Trust." However, if I may offer a tiny critique as a visitor to these shores, there is a slight problem: we don't. Even the best of us can't pull off trusting God properly. That is why it is such a relief to see that Jesus Christ even trusts God for us.

Let me put it like this: my problem is not simply that I am not sufficiently trustworthy—although that may be a problem. It's that I am incapable of exercising trust. And the bad news is that you are incapable as well! We struggle to trust those in our lives who are the most trustworthy; we struggle to trust people who have lavished their love on us for years. More than that, we struggle to trust God himself. In fact, we cannot pull off trusting God, especially not in the long haul. But at last, here in Luke's Gospel, we see One who is both completely trustworthy and One who has the ability to trust perfectly. Here is One who is in control, who is perfectly innocent, and who trusts God perfectly for me.

I hope you can begin to see how Luke skillfully weaves these three related strands into his account of the most moving event in all of history. Jesus stands out in these chapters because he is in control, even when everything appears to be falling apart. Jesus stands out because he is innocent, even when those around him are so determined to condemn him as guilty. Jesus stands out because he trusts God perfectly, even as his friends crumble and his enemies are hell-bent on destroying him.

Sometimes, I suspect, we take Jesus for granted simply because we don't think enough about how awe-inspiring, attractive, complex, and perfect he actually is! We slip into thinking of and speaking of our Lord as if he were one-dimensional, a cardboard cutout. But in this passage, he is anything but that. He is the One in whom all beauty, wisdom, strength, and courage come together. We need to think more about the power, beauty, and majesty of Jesus Christ.

I am not sure anyone captures this incredible complexity of beauty in Jesus better than Jonathan Edwards. In a sermon called "The Excellency of Christ," preached in 1734 and sometimes called "The Admirable Conjunction of Diverse Excellencies in Christ Jesus," Edwards said:

> And here is not only infinite strength and infinite worthiness, but infinite condescension, and love and mercy, as great as power and dignity. If you are a poor, distressed sinner, whose heart is ready to sink for fear that God never will have mercy on you, you need not be afraid to go to Christ, for fear that he is either unable or unwilling to help you. Here is a strong foundation, and an inexhaustible treasure, to answer the necessities of your poor soul, and here is infinite grace and gentleness to invite and embolden a poor, unworthy, fearful soul to come to it. If Christ accepts you, you need not fear but that you will be safe, for he is a strong Lion for your defense. And if you come, you need not fear but that you shall be accepted; for he is like a Lamb to all that come to him, and receives them with infinite grace and tenderness. It is true he has awful majesty, he is the great God, and infinitely high above you; but there is this to encourage and embolden the poor sinner, that Christ is man as well as God; he is a creature, as well as the Creator, and he is the most humble and lowly in heart of any creature in heaven or earth. This may well make the poor unworthy creature bold in coming to him. You need not hesitate one moment; but may run to him, and cast yourself upon him. You will certainly be graciously and meekly received by him.[2]

This is our Lord Jesus Christ: the proper man who is also God; the only innocent One; the One who trusts God; and the sovereign God in the flesh. How can we fail to run to him? How can we take him for granted?

---

[2] *The Works of Jonathan Edwards*, vol. 1 (Edinburgh: Banner of Truth, 1974), 686.

Jesus Stands Out from the People for Whom He Died

Jesus clearly does stand out in these chapters—but not least because of the fact that, as these events unfold, he is surrounded by people like us. Luke includes a "cast of thousands" in his account of Jesus's betrayal and death. More than the other Gospel writers, Luke makes a real effort to give us pictures of the supporting cast members who are standing in the background. He wants us to know about the people who are watching Jesus, who bump into Jesus, and who speak to Jesus. Why does he do it? Luke includes this huge cast of ordinary people to highlight the very simple fact that Jesus dies for *us.*

This Jesus is surrounded by weak people. The disciples are presented as men who are falling apart. Jesus finds that as he wrestles with the reality of providing atonement for people like us, his closest friends are so emotionally exhausted that they fall asleep (22:45). The primary issue here is just their weakness. Jesus's concern for them is that they won't be able to handle what comes next because they are weak—which takes us straight to Peter's weakness.

You've got to admire Peter for following Jesus when the others disappear. But it quickly goes wrong after that—due, clearly, to his weakness. Peter is intimidated by a servant girl who simply says, "This man also was with him" (22:56). On the scale of names called or accusations made, that ranks fairly low. Peter says he doesn't know Jesus (v. 57). When someone says, "You also are one of them," Peter steps up the aggression (v. 58). An hour later, when someone else suggests that he is part of Jesus's entourage, Peter insists, "I do not know what you are talking about" (v. 60). Only hours earlier, he had said, "Lord, I am ready to go with you both to prison and to death" (v. 33). He just can't live up to his good intentions. He's like the rest of us. He's weak. And when he sees his weakness, he goes out and weeps bitterly (v. 62). Even Jesus's best friends are weak—he is surrounded by weak people. People like Peter—and like you and me.

Jesus is surrounded also by evil people. We are given one

picture of Judas: he performs one action, with which he will forever be associated. Judas himself says nothing in Luke's account. But Jesus highlights his betrayal through a kiss of death: "Judas, would you betray the Son of Man with a kiss?" (22:48). Jesus also exposes the evil of Judas's companions, the chief priests and the officers of the temple and the elders: "When I was with you day after day in the temple, you did not lay hands on me" (v. 53). Instead, they have come under cover of night. That's fitting, for Judas's actions and those of the leaders are evil.

In much the same vein, those who hold Jesus mock, beat, and taunt him, and play cruel games with him (22:63–65). Herod and his soldiers humiliate him, treat him with contempt, and dress him up (23:11). The criminal next to him rails against him (v. 39). This is warped. This is evil. This is injustice at its very worst. Jesus is surrounded by evil people. People like Judas, like Barabbas—and like you and me.

It's quite striking that as these world-changing events unfold, the narrative is actually populated by people who act with what can only be described as complete self-interest. Isn't it incredible that this account of God's outrageous self-giving grace is driven along by human self-interest?

Whatever moral qualms Pilate may (or may not) have, it is very clear that the primary motivation for his actions is political self-interest. Luke's verdict is striking: Pilate has already had his political win—he has already gained some credit with Herod—so he says, in effect, "It's not worth my while pursuing justice and losing political capital." He decides that the Jewish leaders' demand should be granted. He releases Barabbas the murderer and delivers Jesus purely out of self-interest (23:24–25).

Herod? Herod wants a magic show (23:8). The events upon which the history of the world revolve are taking place in front of his nose, but he only wants to see some tricks. "Entertain me," he says. When Jesus doesn't perform for him, he turns on him, joining in the mockery of his soldiers (v. 11). It is so childish. The criminal dying beside Jesus yells abuse at him because Jesus won't save him (v. 39). The soldiers just want some extra cash from his clothes (v. 34). While Jesus steels himself to face the wrath of God on our behalf, people are acting selfishly all around him.

In Aberdeen in the north of Scotland, where I studied theology, there is an urban myth that the local newspaper ran the headline "Local Man Lost at Sea" the day after the Titanic went down. It's not actually true. But it could well have been. Like Herod and Pilate, we are desperately self-centered.

I have said some dumb things in my time, but I think that one of the most crass, most cringe-worthy, and most revealing things I have ever said came when I was seventeen. My life was going so well, and then it all came crashing down. I suffered the ultimate humiliation for a seventeen-year-old boy in Northern Ireland—I failed my driving test. There, it's out there. My shame is now a matter of public record. I made the tragic error of taking the test during school time so I could walk back into school a little bit taller, chest puffed out a little more. However, I failed the test. I couldn't bring myself to go back into school and face the public humiliation, so I walked home.

There was no car in the driveway, but to my surprise, I discovered my father sitting there in the living room, looking a bit shaken. Dad was never at home during the day. He explained that he had skidded on black ice on the way to a meeting and crashed, the car was damaged beyond repair, and he had barely avoiding plunging down a ravine into a river. Finally, Dad had narrowly escaped being burned alive as petrol leaked all over him as he made his dazed way from the wreckage.

That's when I said it: "You think you've had a bad day—but I failed my driving test." When Dad gently and graciously tried to point out that I might have things a little out of proportion, I said, "But I have never failed anything." But his fatherly wisdom had clearly survived the accident, as he said simply, "Well, it's about time then!"

I was—am—self-centered, like Herod and Pilate in this narrative. But Luke wants us to see that Jesus dies for people like Herod and Pilate—and like you and me.

But not everyone in the narrative is so obviously self-centered. There are also people who are just oblivious. They have no idea what's going on—nor could they be expected to. The people around the fire who give Peter such a hard time don't know what's happening (22:54–62). Simon of Cyrene doesn't really know what's going on (23:26). The soldiers do what soldiers do, trying to bring some dark humor to their grim job, to pass the time, with no clue about the irony of mocking Jesus as "the King" (vv. 37–38). Many of the crowd who look on have no idea of the significance of the events unfolding before their eyes.

A few years ago, The Edge, the guitarist for the band U2, took his son out "trick or treating" in Los Angeles. Both The Edge and his son dressed in The Edge's trademark black beanie and black leather jacket, with guitars slung around their necks. As they walked away from one front door, they overheard the couple say, "That's a bit sad—that dad doesn't look anything like The Edge!"

Chapters 22 and 23 of Luke are populated by people who are oblivious to the significance of what's unfolding in front of them. People like the soldiers. Like Simon of Cyrene. Like you and me. Some get a little bit but not all of it, such as the men and women who are saddened, probably by the obvious injustice of these events (23:27). As Jesus is shipped from one trial to another, as he is jeered, mocked, beaten, dressed up, and abused, they look on and recoil. This cannot be right! How awful! But Jesus's response to their grief shows they really have no more idea of what's happening than anyone else (vv. 28–31).

There are many people on the planet who show some emotional connection to Jesus's self-sacrifice—who are moved by any representation of Jesus dying on a cross. They know instinctively that this is a bad thing, yet they don't quite get it, at least not yet. But Jesus dies for people like those sad men and women. He dies for people like you and me.

So what's going on here? Why has Luke filled up these chapters with real people—weak people, evil people, self-interested people, oblivious people, and one or two more we'll come to just below? Why has he written his Gospel like this? Why isn't there more on the theology of what's going on?

Actually, this *is* the theology of what's going on. These are real people. This is real folly, real ignorance, real sin. This is fallen humanity. This is why Jesus had to die. In this "cast of thousands," Luke has embedded his theology of substitutionary atonement. Here is one man dying for the ungodly. Here is Jesus Christ.

Luke makes it clear that Jesus dies for people like us. That becomes unmistakable as he describes what happens with Barabbas. The chief priests, the rulers, and the people cry out to Pilate, "Away with this man, and release to us Barabbas," who, Luke says, "had been thrown into prison for an insurrection started in the city and for murder" (23:18–19). Barabbas, a man whose name means "the son of the Father," is released, and the Father's Son, who, in Pilate's words, has done no evil, is chosen to be executed (v. 25). Jesus dies; Barabbas lives. A tragic mistake? No. It is a glorious, deliberate, eternally planned switch. Jesus takes the place of a murderer. One Son of the Father takes the place of others. The One rejected by the mob is chosen by God to save his people. Jesus is dying for us.

If you've read the book *The Hunger Games* or seen the movie, you know that the plot revolves around a horrible contest fought between young representatives of twelve futuristic districts. The contestants in the Hunger Games are forced to kill each another to stay alive, and the winner is the last one standing. The heroine of the book, Katniss Everdeen, is there because she volunteered to take the place of her younger sister, who was selected to represent her district in the games. It is an act of extreme bravery, of real selflessness, of love. But it is utterly understandable: she does this for her little sister. Admirable? Yes. It is the kind of thing that we all hope we would do for our younger siblings, our children, or our spouses.

But Jesus's "substitution" does not work like that. Whose place does Jesus the Messiah take? He takes the place of people like the overwrought disciples and the overreaching Peter. He takes the place of people like the scheming leaders and the spineless governor. He takes the place of people like the bloodstained Barabbas and the cursing criminal. The gospel is ultimately about God and people. It's about us—people for whom Christ died. The people are the reason that Jesus had to drink the cup of God's wrath. We're the reason that Jesus died. How could we ever take this for granted?

Recognizing Jesus

At the end of this deeply moving account, Jesus is finally recognized. For most of this section, it's very obvious that people really don't get who he is, as we've seen. He's not kissed in worship, but kissed in betrayal. Instead of being heeded as the ultimate Prophet, he is told to prophesy for the amusement of the crowd. Instead of being acclaimed as the King of the universe, he is mockingly crowned "King of the Jews." But then he is recognized.

First, he is recognized by a terrorist. Remember, petty felons weren't crucified—only guys like Barabbas. So these are not thieves dying on the cross beside Jesus; they are terrorists. I come from Northern Ireland, where former terrorists are now in the government. That has been hard enough for the nation to get its head around. But how can it be that a terrorist is apparently the first person to recognize what's going on at the center of history? That a terrorist is the first to receive a guaranteed invitation to join Jesus at the table of his heavenly banquet? Yet he is. "And he said, 'Jesus, remember me when you come into your kingdom.' And he said to him, 'Truly, I say to you, today you will be with me in Paradise'" (23:42–43).

This man understands. He gets Jesus's innocence. He gets his own guilt. He understands at some level that Jesus really is the King, despite the clamor of all those around him. And he does the only thing that makes any sense. He asks Jesus to "remember" him. He may not even expect an instant response. It may be a long-term request, aiming for the day when the Messiah sets up the kingdom.

But even as with one ear he hears his friend taunting Jesus, with the other he hears Jesus's words to him: "Today you will be with me in Paradise."

Then Jesus is recognized by the universe he created! In the middle of the day, as Darrell Bock puts it, "the heavens begin to comment."[3] Everything goes dark, the curtain rips, and the cosmos itself recognizes Jesus and the implication of his death (23:44–45).

Finally, after Jesus, using the words of Psalm 31, calls on his Father to resurrect him, astonishingly, a Gentile recognizes him and declares, "Certainly this man was innocent!" (23:47). The centurion realizes that the ultimate switch has taken place. The innocent one has died for the guilty.

Luke wants us to see that Jesus is our substitute. Luke wants us to see that Jesus is the righteous sufferer taking the place of the unrighteous. He wants us to see that Jesus is dying there for us.

It is no accident that this chapter is full of people: weak people, evil people, self-interested people, oblivious people, sad people. The one innocent man is dying for guilty people like this, people like us. The One who is in control, the One who is perfect and innocent, the One who trusts God in a way that we can't is dying for us. He suffers for us, though he is innocent and we are guilty. He trusts for us, even though we are utterly unreliable. He dies for us, even though he is the perfect Son of the Father and we are utterly undeserving.

Luke invites us to stand with these messed-up people and look on Jesus Christ as he is finally recognized by a terrorist, by his Gentile executioner, and by the universe itself. Luke invites us to join them. Luke invites us to see and savor this Jesus; to acknowledge this Jesus as the Lord of the universe, the One to whom we owe everything; to bow before this Jesus, the innocent One who takes our guilt, who brings about his own death that we might live.

This is the heart of the gospel. This is the center of history. This is God dying in our place. How could we take this Jesus for

---

[3] Darrell L. Bock, *Luke*, vol. 2, Baker Exegetical Commentary on the New Testament (Grand Rapids: Baker Books, 2000), 1858.

granted? Romans 5:6–8: "For while we were still weak, at the right time Christ died for the ungodly. For one will scarcely die for a righteous person—though perhaps for a good person one would dare even to die—but God shows his love for us in that while we were still sinners, Christ died for us."

8

JESUS VINDICATED

Luke 24

Tim Keller

This passage is too wonderful for words. But we must try to do it justice. It's very easy to outline this chapter. Everybody does it the same way:

- The empty tomb (vv. 1–12)
- The appearance to the disciples on the road to Emmaus (vv. 13–35)
- The appearance to the disciples in Jerusalem (vv. 36–49)
- The ascension (vv. 50–53)

Or, if you have a certain turn of mind, you could outline it like this: the tomb, the road, the room, the mount.

One way to approach this passage would be to go through it sequentially in sections, just as it's outlined here. However, I would rather give you four themes that run through the sections. In every case, the themes are treated and developed in two or more of the four sections. So let's look at the four messages of this chapter. Those messages are:

1. The resurrection is a shattering historical event.
2. The resurrection is key to understanding all of Scripture.

3. The resurrection gives us a powerful message for the world.

4. Jesus is the true King.

The Resurrection Is a Shattering Historical Event

As a young Christian man, I came up through mainline churches and was a religion major at a secular university. Fairly often, I was given this explanation of the resurrection: after Jesus died, his disciples "experienced" his presence. They felt very powerfully that he was somehow still with them. Peter, for example, experienced forgiveness; he felt that Jesus had really forgiven him for his failures and for his denials. As time went on and the disciples died, their followers began to find ways of expressing these higher truths—these spiritual experiences—through stories that symbolically represented them in concrete form.

So the idea, the "higher truth," that Peter experienced forgiveness from Jesus turned into John 21, where we find the story of Peter meeting Jesus by a fire, Jesus asking him three times, "Do you love me?" and Peter getting Jesus's forgiveness. All of the stories surrounding the resurrection are seen as such symbolic representations of higher spiritual truths. John Dominic Crossan puts it like this: "Emmaus never happened. Emmaus always happens."[1]

In this view, these events are legends. None of them actually happened, yet they always happen, because they tell us about and are symbolic representations of higher spiritual truths. For instance, they reveal the higher truth that "spring always comes after winter," that there's always hope, and that we must hold on to hope.

And yet, when you read through Luke 24, even at the simplest, first-impression level, that explanation just doesn't seem to fit the text.

When he appears among the disciples, Jesus says: "Look at my hands and my feet. It is I myself! Touch me and see; a ghost does not

---

[1] John Dominic Crossan, *The Historical Jesus: The Life and Death of a Mediterranean Jewish Peasant* (San Francisco: HarperSanFrancisco, 1991), xiii.

have flesh and bones, as you see I have" (v. 39).[2] Then he asks, "Do you have anything here to eat?" So they give him a piece of broiled fish, and he eats it (vv. 41–42). Isn't it wonderful how a "higher truth" is being symbolically represented there—Jesus eating fish and chips with the disciples?

But what exactly is this higher truth? The truth of this text is that Jesus is saying: "I'm *not* a symbol. I'm really here. I am not just an impression in your mind. I'm not just a kind of spiritual presence. I'm here, flesh and bones. Feel me. Give me something to eat." You don't write legends like this. Jesus requesting something to eat is almost trivial. It's almost silly. So why is it there? It is there because it happened, because this is what the eyewitnesses actually saw.

The whole chapter has the marks of eyewitness accounts. I'll give you another three examples. You may well have heard these before, but I think they are worth repeating because every time I do, I find that even the most skeptical people have to give them credence.

First, in verses 1–12, we see that the initial witnesses to the empty tomb were women. Women in that day and time had low status, which meant that their testimony was not admissible evidence in court, whether in Roman or Jewish jurisprudence. Therefore, if you were making up a story, if you were creating a legend about the resurrection of Jesus Christ, you would never have put women in there as the first eyewitnesses. It would have done nothing but undermine the plausibility of the account with the hearers or readers of the time. The only possible reason Luke could have had to say women were the first eyewitnesses is that that was what actually happened.

Second, in his great book *Jesus and the Eyewitnesses*, Richard Bauckham asks why there are so many names in this narrative.[3]

---

[2] Scripture references in this chapter are from The Holy Bible, New International Version®, NIV®. Copyright © 1973, 1978, 1984, 2011 by Biblica, Inc.™ Used by permission. All rights reserved worldwide.
[3] Richard Bauckham, *Jesus and the Eyewitnesses* (Grand Rapids: Eerdmans, 2006). See chapter 3, especially pp. 47–55.

Why the names of the women, Joanna and Mary (v. 10)? Cleopas? Why is only Cleopas named and not the other disciple who met Jesus on the road to Emmaus (v. 18)? Why is Luke being so careful? Bauckham points out that in ancient times, these names were like footnotes for a historical account based on eyewitness testimony. It was the historian's way of saying, "If you want to check out what I'm telling you, go talk to these people."

For example, in the book of Mark, Simon of Cyrene, who helped Jesus carry his cross on the way to Calvary, is described as "the father of Alexander and Rufus" (15:21). Alexander and Rufus don't even come into this story. What in the world are their names doing there? The answer, according to Bauckham, is that including them was Mark's way of saying that he got a lot of his information from these two sons. Further, Bauckham shows that there is evidence that Cleopas was probably a very well known eyewitness in the early church for many decades and that he was a significant source of eyewitness accounts.

Third, the most important thing—an amazing thing for me over the years as I was weighing the evidence for the historicity of the resurrection—comes near the very end of the chapter, where Luke says, "Then they worshiped him" (v. 52). As you know, the Gospel accounts were written within the lifetime of many of the eyewitnesses. You may also know that the first accounts of the resurrection and of Jewish Christians worshiping Jesus are from Paul, and, of course, were written much earlier than the Gospels.

If any of you need help falling asleep at night, there's a book called *The Sociology of Philosophies*[4] by Randall Collins, who tries to describe how philosophical and cultural shifts typically happen. Collins says that initially, everyone believes effectively the same thing. Then an outlier comes along and starts to write some outlandish ideas. He's attacked, yet a few people are at least somewhat persuaded. So while the majority, accepted belief stays the same, some people begin to position themselves between the majority and

---

[4]Randall Collins, *The Sociology of Philosophies: A Global Theory of Intellectual Change* (Cambridge, MA: Harvard University Press, 1998).

the outlier, and the center begins to shift. Slowly, over a generation or so, the center is redefined and the majority position changes.

Jews were possibly the least likely people on the face of the earth to be open to the idea that a human being could be God. They had a paradigm, a worldview. They couldn't say the name of God out loud. They couldn't even spell it. Even today they render it as "G-d." Yet we know that almost immediately after the resurrection, Jesus's disciples were worshiping a man. How did that happen? It didn't happen through the sociology of philosophies. It didn't happen through an outlier and slow changes. Oh, no, no, no. Something must have happened. Something must have shattered their paradigm. Only one thing could have done that: they *saw* him. They were confronted with the *fact* of the resurrection.

The resurrection was not preached in the early church as a symbolic representation of higher spiritual truths, something like "We must always keep hope." The resurrection was preached as a hard, bare, terribly irritating, paradigm-shattering, horribly-inconvenient-but-impossible-to-dismiss fact. You know what facts are like. There's a fact. I don't like it. I wish it wasn't there, but it is. What am I going to do about it? I have to accept it. But that isn't the way American culture works. Our culture is about likes and dislikes. It's a Facebook culture: "I like this; I don't like this. I like this; I don't like this."

Paul was the perfect counterexample to today's culture. Paul was deeply offended by Christianity. He was offended by the gospel. For example, he was offended by the idea that people no longer needed a temple. "What? You don't need a temple? You don't need sacrifices for sin? That's outrageous!" He was a Pharisee. He was offended by the very idea of Christianity. But then he saw Jesus raised from the dead. Then his likes and dislikes didn't matter. He didn't care which part he liked or which part offended him anymore. He didn't care anymore because he saw that it was a fact. When it became fact, his earlier opinion no longer mattered.

We really ought to be more sympathetic to our skeptical friends. The resurrection makes Christianity the most irritating religion on the face of the earth. The reason is because many people today decide what they believe by reading it and saying, "I like it" or "I don't like it." Over the years, many people have told me they could never be Christians because there are parts of the Bible they find offensive. Years ago, in my little church in Virginia, people were very offended by what the Bible says about money. Today, in New York, people are much more offended by what the Bible says about sex. They say, "I could never be a Christian."

"Why not?" I ask.

"Well, because there are parts of the Bible I find offensive."

I usually say: "Let me ask you a question. Are you saying that because there are parts of the Bible that you don't like, Jesus Christ couldn't have been raised from the dead?"

"Well, no, I guess I'm not saying that."

And I say: "Every part of the Bible's important, of course, but would you please put the ethical teaching aside for a minute? If Jesus was raised from the dead, you have to deal with everything in the Bible. But if Jesus wasn't raised from the dead, I don't know why you're vexing yourself over any particular ethical teaching."

The fact of the matter is, no matter who you are, Paul was more offended by Christianity than you. He was killing Christians because of how deeply he was offended. But when he realized Jesus had been raised from the dead, it didn't matter what offended him anymore. It didn't matter because Christianity was true. And we have to keep that in mind. The resurrection is a historical event—a paradigm-shattering historical event.

The Resurrection Is Key to Understanding All of Scripture

Near the beginning of this chapter of Luke, angels tell the women to remember what Jesus said: "'The Son of Man must be delivered over to the hands of sinners, be crucified and on the third day be raised again.' Then they remembered his words" (Luke 24:7–8). The resurrection helps them understand Jesus's words. In light of the resurrection, the things that Jesus said aren't quite so crazy.

What happens on the road to Emmaus (vv. 13–35)? Surely this is one of the more comedic parts of the New Testament. The disciples say, "The chief priests and our rulers handed him over to be sentenced to death, and they crucified him; but we had hoped that he was the one who was going to redeem Israel" (vv. 20–21). And Jesus turns around and says, "'How foolish you are, and how slow to believe all that the prophets have spoken! Did not the Messiah have to suffer these things and then enter his glory?' And beginning with Moses and all the Prophets, he explained to them what was said in all the Scriptures concerning himself" (vv. 25–27). The resurrection, when paired with the cross, makes sense of the cross and opens all of Scripture.

In a meditation on Acts 9 in his book *For the Love of God*, Don Carson gives an extremely revealing reconstruction of what might have been going on in Paul's mind when he met the risen Christ.[5] What might Paul have been thinking about during those three days while he was blind?

Saul the Pharisee would have been offended by Christianity for this reason: the Messiah, by definition, is anointed. *Messiah* means "the anointed one," "the chosen one," or "the loved one." The Messiah would please God and would be blessed by God. But Jesus Christ, who was supposed to be the Messiah, died on a cross. The Romans and Jews alike knew that this most ignominious of deaths was the bad end of people who were the lowest of the low. Scripture says, "Cursed is everyone who is hung on a pole" (Gal. 3:13; see Deut. 21:23). Jesus cried out on the cross, "My God, my God, why have you forsaken me?" (Mark 15:34). Maybe Paul didn't know about that, but if he did, it certainly would have gone along with his thinking.

To Paul, Christianity made no sense because the Messiah would be blessed by God, supported by God, and accompanied by God— but Jesus was abandoned by God. He was cursed. "What kind of

---

[5] D. A. Carson, *For the Love of God: A Daily Companion for Discovering the Riches of God's Word*, vol. 1 (Wheaton, IL: Crossway, 1998), July 22.

fool do you take me for?" said Paul. "What kind of salvation could a messiah like that bring?"

Then he saw Jesus raised from the dead.

In the darkness, Paul said something like this to himself: "Wait a minute, if Jesus was raised from the dead, then God *did* vindicate him. Then God *is* pleased with him. Then God *does* love him and has blessed him. And if God does love him and is pleased with him, then when he was cursed and abandoned, he must have been cursed and abandoned for somebody else's sins, not his own."

Then he turned to the rest of the Bible (which, of course, Paul would have carried around in his head). He would have looked at Isaiah, the first part of which shows the Messiah as a great king, but the second half of which is all about this strange figure, the suffering servant. "They couldn't both be the same figure, could they?"

Yes, they could.

Paul looked at Jesus. Then he looked at the temple and the sacrificial system, and said: "Okay, let's think about the whole thing. Did the blood of bulls and goats and little lambs really, over the years, completely atone for sins? That wouldn't make much sense, would it? What if it was pointing to something? What if all that was pointing to Jesus? And if it was all pointing to Jesus, what does that mean about the temple and sacrificial system?"

Then he looked at Ezekiel and Jeremiah, at the passages about a new covenant. It seemed as if God was talking to people face to face and writing the law on their hearts. It was almost as if there was no need for a priest or a temple anymore. What was that new covenant discussion about? How should we understand that?

What about the promise to Abraham—that through Abraham's descendants, all of the nations of the world would be blessed? How would that ever happen?

Uh oh. If Jesus . . . then *this* makes sense. If Jesus . . . then *that* makes sense. If Jesus . . . then *that* makes sense and *that* makes sense.

Do you see what's going on? Once Paul understood the resurrection, he understood the cross. And once he understood the resurrection and the cross together, the whole Bible opened up to him. He had been expecting, as it were, a strong Messiah to come save the strong. His understanding was that the Messiah would come, get up on his horse, and save all those who summoned up their strength to follow him and obey him fully. But instead, he suddenly realized that the Messiah came in weakness to save those who admit their weakness and their need for a Savior. And once he saw that, all of Scripture opened anew.

Jesus is constantly opening minds to the Scriptures. In this instance, we read, "he explained to them what was said in all the Scriptures concerning himself" (v. 27). "Were not our hearts burning within us while he talked with us on the road and opened the Scriptures to us?" (v. 32). "Then he opened their minds so they could understand the Scriptures" (v. 45). And again, "Everything must be fulfilled that is written about me in the Law of Moses, the Prophets and the Psalms. . . . You are witnesses of these things" (vv. 44, 48).

It's not just that the resurrection paired with the cross helps us understand the whole of Scripture. It helps us understand that all of Scripture is about Jesus. Jesus says so. When you preach the Word, whatever part of the Word of God you're expounding, to do it properly you must show how it leads us to understand or see Jesus. This is a big and controversial subject. I am familiar with the pros and cons of the arguments, but when all is said and done, Jesus seems to be saying here that it's all about him. Once you see the resurrection and the cross, you see that it's all about him.

I don't think that means, by the way, that every single verse is really about Jesus. I love the way Don Carson handles this in his exegesis of the parable of the good Samaritan (see chapter 4). Who is the good Samaritan? He is an unexpected savior because it's a Jewish man lying in the road. The Jews and the Samaritans have nothing but hostility between them, but along comes a Samaritan who, at the risk of his own life, stops to rescue a man who would have expected the opposite. When Jesus gives the parable of the good Samaritan, is he really saying that he is the good Samaritan?

Is he actually trying to convey that this is his work, that this is a symbolic figure of him? Don says no; that's clearly not what he is trying to do. However, when you realize how Luke himself winds his themes together and takes us to the cross, and that all aspects of salvation, all aspects of rescue, all those plotlines in the Bible converge in Jesus Christ, how can you not see Jesus in the good Samaritan? Jesus is the ultimate unexpected Savior who comes— not just at the risk of his life, but at the cost of his life—and gives you the opposite of not just what you should expect, but what you deserve.

If you have seen the movie *The Sixth Sense*, you know that you can see that movie only twice. The first time you see it, you find out that there is a big, shocking ending. The second time you see it, you can't possibly see any earlier part of the movie without thinking about the end. Once you know the end—I don't want to spoil it for you, but Bruce Willis is dead—everything that comes earlier takes on new meaning. So the second time you see the movie, you watch Willis's character with his wife, and you say: "They're in the same room, and they're both talking, and the first time I thought they were talking to each other. Now I realize she doesn't ever really look at him." Because you know the ending, you can't *not* look at every scene in light of that ending. It's impossible.

I could be practical about this. My wife, Kathy, years ago helped me understand this when she said: "You know, honey, your sermons tend to be like Sunday school lessons until you get to Jesus. They're very informative and people are taking notes. But when you get to Jesus"—if I remember correctly, she probably said, "But *if* you get to Jesus . . ."—"it becomes a real sermon. Everybody puts their pens and pencils down, and everybody just soars." Even to this day, that is still the number one way in which she decides whether you have a Sunday school lesson or a sermon, whether you're instructing people in the minutia of the text or actually preaching the Bible, preaching the Gospel, and preaching Jesus.

John Calvin put it this way:

He [Christ] is Isaac, the beloved Son of the Father who was offered as a sacrifice, but nevertheless did not succumb to the power of death. He is Jacob the watchful shepherd, who has such great care for the sheep which he guards. He is the good and compassionate brother Joseph, who in his glory was not ashamed to acknowledge his brothers, however lowly and abject their condition. He is the great sacrificer and bishop Melchizedek, who has offered an eternal sacrifice once for all. He is the sovereign lawgiver Moses, writing his law on the tables of our hearts by his Spirit. He is the faithful captain and guide Joshua, to lead us to the Promised Land. He is the victorious and noble king David, bringing by his hand all rebellious power to subjection. He is the magnificent and triumphant king Solomon, governing his kingdom in peace and prosperity. He is the strong and powerful Samson, who by his death has overwhelmed all his enemies.

This is what we should in short seek in the whole of Scripture: truly to know Jesus Christ, and the infinite riches that are comprised in him and are offered to us by him from God the Father. If one were to sift thoroughly the Law and the Prophets, he would not find a single word which would not draw and bring us to him. [. . .] Therefore, rightly does Saint Paul say in another passage that he would know nothing except Jesus Christ, and him crucified.[6]

The Resurrection Gives Us a Powerful Message for the World

It seems obvious, as we read Luke 24, that the minute people find out about the resurrection, they communicate it to others. Nobody sits on this message. Immediately after the women meet the angels, they come back from the tomb and tell all these things to the eleven (v. 9). The Emmaus disciples come back at once and tell the eleven and those with them what they have seen (vv. 33–35). And, of course, Jesus himself says, "This is what is written: The Messiah

---

[6] Preface to Pierre Robert Olivétan's translation of the New Testament, 1534. This text, from the *Opera, C. R. 9*, pp. 791ff., contains additions Calvin made after 1534. Cited from Joseph Haroutunian, *Calvin: Commentaries* (Westminster John Knox Press, 1958), 69.

will suffer and rise from the dead on the third day, and repentance for the forgiveness of sins will be preached in his name to all nations, beginning at Jerusalem. You are witnesses of these things" (vv. 46–48). Of what things? The resurrection. Knowing about the resurrection gives you a message to take to the world.

To be clear, I'm not pressing the idea that the resurrection, all by itself, without anything else, is the main message. No, the resurrection paired with the cross is the powerful message. However, when you read the rest of the book of Acts, it is astounding how the resurrection dominates the preaching of Peter and Paul. Those early preachers cannot stop talking about the resurrection.

One of the more interesting historical questions is how Christianity, within two or three centuries, was able to completely supplant the classical culture of the Greco-Roman world. We still study the great philosophers because they were brilliant. Some people say all modern Western thought is just a series of footnotes on Plato. That is certainly an exaggeration, but it shows how influential the Greco-Roman philosophers were. How is it possible that within a relatively short time, the populace turned away from paganism, away from classical culture, and embraced Christianity. How did it happen?

I'm interested whenever a historian or somebody who's not a Christian tries to explain it. I even tend to trust their objectivity a little bit more. Lately, some of those I have been reading say it was the resurrection. The resurrection was unique. The resurrection was a kind of message no one in the Greco-Roman world had ever heard, and it gave deep hope for the future—that the future is here, that it's personal, that it's certain, and that it's unimaginably wonderful. It still does all that today.

First, the future is here. Epicurus, one of the great Greek philosophers, believed that when you die, that's it—you're gone. There's no sensation; when you die, you won't even know it. Therefore, there's nothing to be afraid of. Although most of the common people believed in an afterlife, it was more of a shadowy underworld, and nobody knew for sure that it was all that great a place anyway.

Many of the Jews weren't sure about the afterlife either. The Saddu-cees certainly didn't believe in the resurrection and perhaps didn't believe in any afterlife at all.

But regardless of who you were, Jew or Gentile, if you talked to an eyewitness of the resurrection, saw his changed life, and be-lieved the credibility of his account, finally you knew that you were not just dust in the wind. Finally you knew that you were not just a stone that would eventually sink to the bottom. Finally you knew there is a future. The resurrection proved it.

Second, the future is not just here, it's personal. The Stoics were like Eastern philosophers, saying that when you die you continue to exist, but not as your personal self. You become part of the All Soul. You become part of the substance of the world: So there's no reason to be afraid.

I continually hear people today say that when you die, that's it, you simply cease to exist, or that when you die, you become part of the universe, part of the circle of life—you become part of the fertilizer, and out of that come plants that other living things eat, and so you become part of the world. Either way, there's no reason to be afraid of death.

But be honest. Without the Holy Spirit, the deepest desire of the human heart is to be loved: we want to be with our loved ones. The one thing we do not want is to lose our loved ones—to have a love that we lose. Most people know that love is the thing that gives meaning in life.

So how can anyone say that when you die there is nothing to be afraid of—while everything that matters to you is being stripped away, while death has taken your loved ones while you lived and eventually takes you from your loved ones when you die? What solace is there in saying that, when you die, you don't know any-thing or that you become part of the universe, that you don't have your personality?

No, Jesus Christ shows up in resurrected form and says: "It is I, myself. Look at me. Here are my wounds. It's me." Your future is personal, and that is the only thing that can satisfy the human heart. Don't say that you're not afraid of death if you don't believe in the resurrection or an afterlife in which you're personal in some way. That's too brutal to be honest.

Third, the future is certain, and that is essential. What good is it to be told without certainty that there is a personal future surrounded by love without parting—a future with no end to the love of the Father, the love of Jesus Christ, and the love of others? What consolation does such a future provide if you are uncertain it is for you?

Martin Luther said suffering is intolerable if you are unsure of your salvation, unsure that, in spite of all of your flaws, God is with you. That is, suffering is intolerable in the face of an uncertain future. But your future can be certain because of the resurrection. Here are a couple of ways to think about this.

Suppose you are sentenced to jail for breaking the law. The day you get out of jail, that law has no more claim on you; the debt has been paid. The wages of sin is death (Rom. 6:23). Jesus Christ went into death, and when he came up out of the grave, that meant the debt was paid. The resurrection is how you know it was paid.

You could also think of the resurrection as a receipt. Suppose you buy something at a department store, and as you are walking out the door, a plainclothes security person stops you and says, "Excuse me, may I look in your bag?" You hold up your receipt and say: "O plainclothes security person, trouble me not! This receipt proves my item has been paid for, and I do not have to pay for it again." The resurrection is a giant receipt, stamped across history, for all people to see. The resurrection says that you can know your future is certain if you believe in Jesus Christ.

Fourth, the resurrection does not tell you only that the future is there, that it's personal, and that it's certain, but also that it's unimaginably wonderful. Here's the reason why.

Edgar Allen Poe's most famous literary work is probably "The Raven." It's a very strange poem, a very dark poem. It's about a man who is bereaved; he has lost his love, a woman named Lenore, and he's trying to figure out whether he will ever be happy again.

Then a raven comes in and sits on a bust of Pallas, and keeps saying one word over and over again: "Nevermore." That word gets across, with frightening pithiness, what life is about, or at least what it seems to be about—the irreversibility of life. When things are gone, they're gone, and they are seemingly irretrievable.

When you get old, your youth seemingly is gone forever. When my wife, Kathy, was growing up, she had the most wonderful time of her life every summer for two weeks at a little compound of rickety cottages on the shores of Lake Erie. But now, the cottages are gone. In fact, that part of the beach is gone. It's all gone, and whenever she goes back there, she just weeps. It's irretrievable. She'll never get it back.

In some ways, this kind of irretrievability is like a death in the midst of life, and the older you get, the more it can suck all the joy out of your life. When I lose something, it's gone; it's just gone. But do you realize what the resurrection is? Even religions that promise you a kind of spiritual future, spiritual bliss, offer only consolation for what you've lost. But the resurrection is the *restoration* of what you've lost. You don't just get your body back; you get the body you always wanted but never had. You don't just get your life back; you get the life you always wanted but never had.

I know there are people in my church who have chosen not to marry anyone who cannot be a true spiritual partner, and because they are faithful in that way, they will probably never get married. What should they say? "I'll never have that. I'll never have that joy. I'm too old. Nobody will marry me now. I've lost it forever. It's gone. 'Nevermore.'" No. Jesus Christ is resurrected proof that you will miss nothing. There will be a wedding feast—real wine, real arms—and it will be your wedding feast.

What about those of you locked in bad marriages? You're simply trying to keep it together and face the reality that you will probably never have the great experiences you see in the flourishing marriages of others. Should you just say that you will never have that, that your opportunity is irretrievably gone? No, the resurrection means you will miss nothing—absolutely nothing. It's all coming in the future, and it will be unimaginably wonderful.

There is no religion, no faith, no philosophy, and no person who has ever offered the world this kind of future—a future that is there, personal, certain, and unimaginably wonderful. There's no more powerful message possible, and it is a message based on the historical fact of the resurrection. If you don't like this or that ethical teaching of the Bible, look at that future. Don't you want that? Even if you are not a Christian, wouldn't you want that kind of future to be true? You have to want that. You're not being honest with yourself if you say you don't want that.

Jesus Is the True King

Here's the last thing to say. Jesus Christ twice calls himself the Messiah. Once he says: "How foolish you are, and how slow to believe all that the prophets have spoken! Did not the Messiah have to suffer these things and then enter his glory?" (Luke 24:25–26). And then, "This is what is written: The Messiah will suffer and rise from the dead on the third day, and repentance for the forgiveness of sins will be preached in his name to all nations" (vv. 46–47). Isn't it interesting that, at the very end, Jesus refers to himself using not the word *I* but the word *Messiah*, which, of course, refers to the King. That's how he goes out: "I'm the King. I'm the true King."

John Guest is an Anglican minister who moved to this country from Britain in the early 1970s. Visiting a museum of some sort here in the United States, he was looking at various Revolutionary War memorabilia. He noticed a big sign that had been put up on a tavern in Philadelphia during the Revolution. It said, "We serve no sovereign here." That's when he realized he was in a new country.[7] Even Australians, Canadians, and Europeans have some positive memory of bowing the knee. Asians also see the benefits and the appropriateness of respecting authority. But we Americans declare, "We serve no sovereign here." We don't bow the knee to anybody. We

---

[7] R. C. Sproul, *The Prayer of the Lord* (Orlando, FL: Reformation Trust, 2009), 40–41.

are individuals, and we decide what is right or wrong for each of us. And this sensibility of ours is spreading throughout the world.

C. S. Lewis wrote a little article some years ago called "Equality." In it, he says he is absolutely in favor of democracy—because we are all sinners. And because we are all sinners, we need checks and balances. However, he says, democracy is medicine, not food. Ultimate reality is not democracy. We were made to be ruled, and if you don't acknowledge Jesus as King, you will serve somebody else. You will bow the knee to someone or something. You may not admit that is what you are doing, but human nature will be served. If it doesn't get food, it'll gobble poison. You need a king. You will serve somebody.

Jesus is your King. Obey him. That is, treat him as a King. Do whatever he says, whether you like it or not. Trust him. Accept what he sends into your life, whether you understand it or not. Rely on him. Don't say you believe in Jesus while you are really getting all of your self-worth out of your career. That means your career is king.

Make Jesus your King and expect great things from him. Treat him like a King in prayer. Do you know how to do that? John Newton says:

Thou art coming to a King,
Large petitions with thee bring;
For His grace and power are such,
None can ever ask too much.[8]

Jesus is the King.

---

[8] From the hymn "Come, My Soul, Thy Suit Prepare" by John Newton, 1779.

Appendix

DID JESUS PREACH THE GOSPEL?

Conference Panel

D. A. Carson, Kevin DeYoung, Tim Keller, John Piper

On one evening of The Gospel Coalition 2013 National Conference, an important public conversation took place. We present that conversation here, even though the live dynamics cannot be captured in print. Not often enough does the larger church have an opportunity to listen in on conversations among evangelical leaders as they try to guard the good deposit. Here the theme is "Jesus and the Gospel," the central question being the relationship between Jesus's preaching and Paul's preaching, especially in regard to the concept of kingdom.

We've only slightly edited the discussion, for several reasons. First, what was happening was not a polished presentation, but rather real-time interaction and genuine enlightenment on the topic. We wanted to maintain both the "realness" and the energy of that process—not to mention the fact that it might encourage all the rest of us to hear some almost convoluted sentences come from the mouths of these men as they're being vulnerable enough to think out loud in front of a crowd of thousands. Second, their personalities come through as they interact: Don Carson is the professorial pastor-leader who isn't afraid to put the word *complexify* on the table—or to push the others to consider the topic from a different angle. Kevin DeYoung is young, humble, and unafraid to speak straight—and always straight from Scripture. Tim Keller is honest and full of challenging ideas he's read or considered—or is just now thinking of. John Piper is passionate and piercing. They are quite distinctly who they are—and they listen to and like each other well.

Finally, we reproduce the discussion as it happened because these men were together getting at the most crucial stuff of our faith: the person and work of Jesus Christ, and the inspired and inerrant Scriptures. We at The Gospel Coalition offer this discussion as one that might, by God's grace, encourage the church to focus with increasing clarity on the gospel of Jesus, the King who died to save us, the resurrected King who reigns, and the coming King whose kingdom is both here and coming, on earth as it is in heaven.

Kathleen B. Nielson

D. A. Carson (DAC): I am going to begin by asking the question that sets up all the rest of the discussion. To some in this hall, the question must seem odd: "Did Jesus preach the gospel?" What prompts this question today? What studies or books or trends or assumptions or movements are driving this question?

Tim Keller (TK): I did not come out of an evangelical background. I went to a mainline church growing up, became a Christian in college, and found myself often listening to a different kind of Christianity. We're talking about the late sixties and early seventies in, I guess, what you might call the mainline churches. And generally what I heard there was—I think John and Don will be able to correct me if I'm saying this improperly—the idea of Ernst Käsemann and many others, what you might call more liberal scholars, that Jesus preached the kingdom. That's the heart of what Christianity is all about. It has a social justice aspect. It has an eschatological aspect. That's really what Christianity is about—about this future kingdom. It has broken in now. We need to be, in a sense, witnesses in some way to that in-breaking kingdom by the way in which we live our lives. That usually meant calling for social justice. And the more traditional idea—the more traditional evangelical ministry of calling people to be born again and calling people to be converted—was considered individualistic, narrowly focused on various Pauline Epistles. And that's the Christianity I rejected when I went to Gordon-Conwell and I considered myself a Reformed evangelical. Today I hear more and more people inside the evangelical world saying the same sorts of things—pitting the preaching of Jesus in the Synoptics and the preaching of the kingdom against preaching a gospel of (what would be called) individualistic eternal life: simply getting your born-again certificate, knowing you're forgiven, and living out your life and going to heaven. Today those things are pitted against each other inside the evangelical world. And I'm pretty sure that many of the people who use this same terminology don't mean quite the same thing as those liberals I heard in my youth. I think they are probably more orthodox. . . . And yet, I would say it's actually a bit troubling to me that things that probably should be integrated are being pitted against each other. Now that's the reason why, when I saw the topic, I thought, yes, we definitely have to address that.

DAC: I know you've got an example or two. Go ahead.

Kevin DeYoung (KD): Well, I just figured I should let John Piper speak first, but . . .

You know, I was reading a book on the plane down here—a good book in many ways. In the last chapter, however, the author argues (and admittedly he says it's a bit of a provocative thesis) for a canon within the canon, and that the Gospels really ought to be that canon through which we make sense of the rest of the Bible. I'll just read a few sentences, because I think this will be illustrative of what we're trying to address, at least in part. So he says:

The Gospels—and in reality, the life and teachings of Jesus—have often played only a secondary and subsidiary role. The real bread and butter of our Christian experience, teaching, and worldview formation has come from the Epistles and orthodox doctrine. A focus on the death of Jesus (and to a lesser degree his resurrection) has been the extent to which the Jesus traditions have impacted our thought, but even this is primarily mediated through the Epistles' summations and applications. The actual life and teachings of Jesus have not been the center.

Then I'll just read the contrast several pages later. If we start with the Epistles,

... we may get a somewhat skewed picture of the main point of the new covenant. This does not mean that our perspective will necessarily be erroneous or incompatible but rather slightly unbalanced. For example, as is typical in much of the Protestant tradition, the eschatological kingdom of God is not a major theme when "the gospel" is discussed, but rather justification by faith or something similar. But when we begin with Jesus's own teaching and the focus of the Gospels, we can rightly read and understand the rest of the New Testament as an outworking and application . . . of this same perspective.[1]

That is from a book that, for the most part, I appreciate, but I got to the end of that chapter and thought, "Hmm, that seems relevant to what we're trying to discuss on this panel." And it has to do with just what you said: Are we in error in evangelical circles? Have we gone in some imbalanced direction so that, in fact, we're reading everything through Paul? And what are the problems even with the way I just asked that question—that somehow we've got Paul and then we have Jesus. And we know who's going to win that one.

---

[1] Jonathan T. Pennington, *Reading the Gospels Wisely: A Narrative and Theological Introduction* (Grand Rapids: Baker Academic, 2012), 233, 252.

John Piper (JP): The problem I have with that is that "start" feels so irrelevant. "Start." "If you *start* with Jesus . . ." "If you *start* with Paul . . ." I don't care where a person starts. I want to know where they end. In other words, I want to know, after you've read both of them, what do you believe about them? What do you understand? Who cares whether you read Luke first or Romans first or Colossians first? This temporal hermeneutical trick is odd to me. My brain doesn't work that way. And I think this objection is pretty profound. In other words, we ought to read the Gospels and to read the Epistles, and to understand them both for what they are. And it doesn't matter which one we start with. We should understand Jesus's message. Does it cohere wonderfully with Paul's? Does Paul's cohere wonderfully with Jesus's? Does each bring to bear on us what we need to know for life and godliness? And so I'm not helped by saying we would do well if we started with Jesus because then we would read Paul in the best light. Ah, my guess is that the Galatians read Galatians first, and then they might have seen Luke.

TK: I'm sure the Corinthians read Corinthians first. No, I think that when people say, "Start with the Gospels," I think what they are saying is that traditional evangelicalism has tended to read the Gospels through Paul, that Paul is more fundamental. Paul gives us the basic categories. And Paul colors our reading of the Gospels. And this writer [whom Kevin DeYoung quoted] wants to reverse that. He wants the Gospels to give us the categories and see Paul as the outworking of that. . . . The charge we have to refute or we have to at least answer is the charge that traditional evangelicalism reads the Gospels in light of Paul. I just think . . . two wrongs don't make a right. If we are using Paul and in a sense muting the distinctives of the Gospels, then we shouldn't turn the tables. And it seems to me that they should be mutually informing. I've always believed, like I think all of us, that when you're interpreting the Scripture, the clear parts should inform the murkier parts. If you get to some places in the Bible that are kind of murky, you don't choose your own particular interpretation of that and then be so sure you're right that you go back and reread the rest of the Bible in light of it. You take the clear parts and you use those to understand the murky parts. But Paul's not murky; the Gospels aren't murky. They should be mutually informing. And I really don't like the idea—again, I think that's what they mean by "starting"—of trying to give one part of the Bible pride of place.

DAC: Partly hidden behind the question is the fact that, while the Bible is the product of God's blessed inspiration, it is his Word, yet, God has given his Word through human beings in particular situations, in particular kinds of literature, particular times and places, and so forth. The way the whole thing has been cast focuses purely on that historical plane. In that case, there are some questions to be asked, for example, about how Paul's vocabulary is different from, say, Luke's. Perhaps we'll come to some of those things. But behind all of it is the reality that God gave it all. And it's not as if one part of it is more the Word of God than another part of it. And so, you want to phrase the questions in such a way that, if all of it is the Word of God, if there is one mind behind all of it and you want to find the one mind behind it, your job is to integrate it all rather than break it apart on these historical planes and give one part some sort of a privileged status.

JP: And before we work hard, if we do, to rescue the Gospels, because we evangelicals emphasize Paul, who's to say, Mr. So-and-so, that when you read a sequence of documents—some founding events and others' interpretative consummative events—that the second wouldn't and shouldn't be the one through which you read the first one? I mean, if I wrote a book, that's the way I would want you to do it. Read the whole book—oh, got it! Now, let's go back to get it. That's the way I'd want people to do it. . . . Now, I'm going to retreat from that and say, read Luke for Luke. Let Luke have his say. Read Romans for Romans. Let Paul in Romans have his say. But if God did inspire all these twenty-seven books, and if he did order, in his providence, that they come into being and be ordered in the way we find them in the New Testament, and if he did say, in effect, "I will bring to your remembrance all things," and put in place an apostolate who would then instruct his church how to interpret his life: Why wouldn't you let Paul have a pretty strong say in what you do with the way we read the Gospels? I would ask that person that question.

KD: And getting what both of you said—when Jesus promises that the Holy Spirit will come and lead you into "all truth"—of course, we have to read that contextually. It's not all truth about whom you're going to marry and where you're going to live and what your major is—it's all truth about Jesus Christ and his glory and bringing these things to mind, so that the inspired apostolic record after the events of Jesus's life and death and resurrection should have a bearing on how we understand it, because that's the work of the Spirit. And I think you were hitting on it, Don, when you suggested that tied up in some of this is a view of inspiration common at a more popular level. You see this with the frequent attempts to be red-letter Christians. I mean, that just comes up and recycles every five or ten years. I'm not that old and I've seen that thing come or go two or three times. Okay, there's Paul. Okay. But we've got Jesus's words. And how often do you hear, just in media outlets, "Well, Jesus never said anything about—that was just Paul later." And that totally betrays what we ought to believe about the unity of the Scriptures, that all Scripture is breathed out by God.

DAC: I'd like to point out, just to reassure everyone here, that John Piper actually believes that there are sixty-six books, not just twenty-seven. Just in case there is any doubt in anybody's mind.

JP: To follow up here.

DAC: Sure. Then, we'll go on to the next question.

JP: Not to that. That stands. That's true.

TK: He's going to ignore that.

JP: Why would we expect that the Lord Jesus in coming into the world to die—"I came to die," he said in more ways than one—why would we assume that his preparatory talking before the performance of salvation would somehow be anywhere near as normative about the nature of the salvation as what follows? In other words, it seems to me that it's inherently to be expected that before salvation is performed at Good Friday and Easter, one would speak of salvation a bit differently than after it had been performed and now all could be seen in light of the performance of why he came, and therefore, the postdiscussion of it authoritatively after the performance would be different. That would just be what I would expect. And so, I don't, again, get it why one would elevate the preperformance articulation of salvation to the postperformance articulation of salvation.

DAC: Let me push just a wee bit on the difference of vocabulary just the same. How do we respond to those who say that Paul preaches the gospel? *The gospel* is a big word with him. One could mention a whole list of words that are pretty common in Paul that are not nearly as common in the four canonical Gospels. And meanwhile, there is an emphasis on kingdom especially in the Synoptic Gospels that is not as prominent in Paul. So the question that some critics ask is, "What do we make of the fact that Paul preaches the gospel while Jesus preaches the kingdom?" In other words, we are dealing now with texts and not just with assumptions.

TK: Well, I have a question for you. I know that's not fair. You just asked the question. But Don is one of the great Johannine scholars in the world. I think it's a little interesting that when they say, "In the Gospels, you have the kingdom, kingdom, kingdom. In Paul, the word *kingdom* doesn't come up very much," but they are forgetting that one of the Gospels, the Gospel of John, hardly uses the word *kingdom*. And in fact, I really wonder why that approach shows such disrespect to the Gospel of John. It gives you the impression that Jesus in his own ministry would never have preached the gospel as it were, would never have given people the good news without talking about the kingdom, but in the Gospel of John, he only uses the term *kingdom* in his own language twice. One is with Nicodemus, but okay . . . well, you're the John scholar.

DAC: Three times. Twice with Nicodemus and once in John 18.

TK: When he was talking with Pilate—where's the other one?

DAC: Twice with Nicodemus and once with Pilate in John 18.

TK: I knew that.

DAC: Hey, this is why they pay me the big bucks.

TK: I was considering that twice, but anyway . . .

DAC: And they all with one accord began to make excuse.

TK: That seems to give lie to the assumption. This is the first time I've put it in my mind this way. The assumption seems to be that using the term *kingdom* is the superior way to preach the Christian message, and that if you don't use the term, because Jesus uses the term, other ways are somehow deficient. And yet, you have one of the four Gospels in which Jesus doesn't ordinarily use the term *kingdom*. It seems almost like eternal life—I'll test my hypothesis with this John scholar—eternal life seems to almost be in the place of the kingdom. John seems to talk about eternal life so much more. So that again seems to me to get rid of this idea that somehow the Synoptic preaching of Jesus is the peak and everything else is downhill from there. What do you think, Mr. John Scholar?

DAC: Historically, you are entirely right. That is to say, most of those who insist on the primacy of kingdom language for the historical Jesus end up either implicitly or explicitly depreciating the value of John's Gospel for understanding the historical Jesus— claiming that it all has to be dismissed as later theological reflection rather than something that is a faithful witness to the historical Jesus. And so, you end up not only depreciating Paul, you end up depreciating John. Then, if you push a little further because you observe some sort of Synoptic dependence, you might assert Markan priority. And then, at the end of the day, the supreme record for getting at the historical Jesus is Mark. And thus, you're not only having a canon within the canon. If you're not careful, you're having a canon within a canon within a canon within the canon. That kind of reductionism, at the end of the day, surely has to make anybody nervous who thinks that God has given us *sixty-six* books!

JP: Kevin has something to say! He's got his Bible open.

TK: Say something Kevin!

KD: I'm thinking of Mark because Mark begins in verse 1, "The beginning of the gospel of Jesus Christ, the Son of God." There's the title page. This is going to be a book about the gospel of Jesus Christ, so a pretty good indication that we're going to learn something about the gospel here. And the very first thing out of Jesus's mouth in Mark's Gospel is: "The time is fulfilled. The kingdom of God is at hand. Repent and believe in the gospel." And whether you understand those two clauses to be equivalent, at least they're explanatory of each another, leaning into each other. "The kingdom of God is at hand." This heavenly reign and rule of God is breaking in in the person of Christ. And then what? "Repent and believe." Now it doesn't seem a stretch to me that you start to sound very Pauline very quickly. We're talking about repentance, we're talking faith—that's also John's language more than any other, with faith—and then, by Mark 2, Jesus is healing the paralytic. He says, "Son, your sins are forgiven." So it seems to be uppermost in his mind that the gospel has at its center the forgiveness of sins. And then, at the end, when he calls Levi—and what we saw this morning in the parallel passage—"It's not those who are well who have need of a physician, but those who are sick. I came not to call the righteous, but sinners." And you could go through Mark's Gospel, which is supposed to be the quintessential example of this kind of kingdom language, to show that part and parcel of the kingdom is calling people—not to *do* (though there are lots of commands Jesus gives), but the verbs related to the kingdom are verbs of inheritance, reception, entering in, receiving. You're receiving this gift through faith and repentance. And that to me sounds like not only what the gospel is in Mark, but what we preach when we come to Romans and Galatians and Philippians.

DAC: Now I know that you guys did some preparation for this and you looked up some material on the kingdom in Paul that I thought was really helpful. And I know that you did some reading in books on the subject. Would you like to talk about those things in reference to this question? How do we think about this charge that at the end of the day the vocabulary differences are just so notable that you have to think in different categories? Kevin has introduced the subject; go further.

JP: Right. If you simply judge by proportion, you have ninety-some mentions of *gospel*, and thirteen to fourteen references to *kingdom* in the Epistles not insignificant references. Romans: "kingdom is righteousness, joy, and peace." First Corinthians: "kingdom is not talk but power," "he will not inherit the kingdom," "he must reign until he puts all of his enemies under his feet, then he hands the kingdom over to the Father." And many more—seven or eight more. So kingdom language is not missing.

Here's my take on the reason for the disproportion, and you tell me what you think. Jesus intentionally did not preach Jesus as explicitly as Paul preaches Jesus. In fact, he hid Jesus—"Don't tell anybody." And you in your talk alluded to why: namely, they didn't have a clue what real Messiah was and real kingdom was, so Jesus was gradually reinterpreting Messiah, reinterpreting kingdom, and he winds up stretched out on a cross as King—"Are you the king?" "You say that I am and now I'm reaching my goal." Dead. So Jesus is gradually deconstructing kingdom; transforming kingdom; lowering kingdom—"The rulers of this earth lord it over those, but I am among you as one who serves." Think kingdom. So he's reinterpreting kingdom and concealing himself, as it were, temporarily until he does his work. And when Paul comes along, he preaches Christ—"We preach Christ as Lord." So in my understanding, Paul perfectly understood what Jesus was doing in reinterpreting kingdom, making himself ready to be the crucified, truly understood Messiah King. "And now I don't preach that kingdom anymore as often; I preach Christ the King, and then kingdom is brought in subordinately." So Jesus foregrounds it and reinterprets it. Paul backgrounds it and puts the King, Jesus, in the foreground, which is just what, I think, Jesus would want him to do and what makes sense that he should do.

DAC: That's hugely helpful. You've got some really good stuff there.

TK: Yes, I don't have anything as hugely helpful as that, I don't think, honestly. That is very helpful to me, too. The reason I actually brought up the Gospel of John is I think it's intriguing to see ways in which, if you go back and forth between John and the Synoptics, you don't want to say they're exactly synonymous, but the terms "inherit eternal life," "enter the kingdom of God," "be saved," "to turn or to be converted" are used in very similar ways. So one example is in Mark 10 (and, of course, Matthew 19 and Luke). The rich young ruler asks Jesus what must he do to inherit eternal life, and when he goes away discouraged, Jesus doesn't say, "Oh, it's really hard for the rich to get eternal life." He could have, but instead he says, "It's hard for those with wealth to enter the kingdom of God." It almost looks like they're the same thing. Another interesting spot would be if you take a look at Matthew 18:3: "Truly, truly I say to you," Jesus says, "unless you turn"—some translations say "unless you're converted"—"and become like children, you will never enter the kingdom of heaven." John 3:3 says, "Truly, truly, I say to you, unless one is born again," verse 5, "he cannot enter the kingdom of God." And the parallels—I would love to hear from my brothers here—I don't believe they are complete synonyms. I don't think God would have the different terms unless each term brought out, maybe, a different aspect.

But what brought this all together was years ago reading George Ladd's *Theology of the New Testament*, and Ladd says that here is what brings it all together—eternal life is future life brought into the present now through faith in the work of Jesus Christ. So when I believe in Jesus Christ, eternal life doesn't mean just simply that now I know that I'll live forever because I am forgiven. Eternal life is a quality of life from the future that comes in now. Dick Gaffin was also very good at talking about that. You know he brings out the fact that *palingenesia*, the renewal of all things in Matthew 19, is also the word Paul uses in Titus for what happens in you. When he talks about regeneration, he uses a word that means the renewal of all things at the end of time, and also what renews you now when you are born again. So what always helped me enormously was to say kingdom life is eternal life. It's the life of the future come in now, which I get through faith in Christ. It's "already" but "not yet." It's here partially. I'm partly renewed, but it's surely not fully here yet because it's a down payment on the future. That draws it all together, and it's one of the reasons why in John you don't need to use *the kingdom* necessarily. I believe everything that John Piper just said about why it could be that kingdom terminology actually seems to fade a bit with Paul. And maybe you could even see it in John since John is the last of the Gospels to be written. Maybe it's not necessary to background Jesus anymore. I think that's actually quite helpful. But just the idea that eternal life is the future life of the kingdom now has always drawn it all together for me, and it makes it impossible for me to see why we're pitting these against each other—why we have to say the kingdom language of the Synoptics has to take precedence over what Paul says.

DAC: Is there any sense at all in which it is helpful to talk about the gospel of Paul, the gospel of justification, the gospel of the kingdom? I mean, the expression "the gospel of the kingdom" is found, of course, in the Synoptics. Is it helpful for us to use those expressions today? The gospel of the kingdom? The gospel of Paul? The gospel of justification? Or whatever? And if so, in what ways can we properly use them and in what ways must we not use them?

JP: You tweeted about this yesterday.

KD: I did?

JP: Or today? According to and of. That's relevant.

KD: Oh, I did? Good.

JP: You want me to remind you what you said?

KD: No. I do remember now. Well, you look in your Bible and it will say "The Gospel according to Mark." And you've talked about this a number of times, Don. "The Gospel according to Matthew." That there's a reason it's not "The Gospel *of*"—Mark's got a gospel and John's got a gospel and, well, maybe they worked together, who knows? It was a deliberate understanding of the early church that there was one story. There was one narrative. There was one storyline of good news. And these four Gospels are giving it, according to Mark. So here Mark's going to give his angle, but it's the one gospel. It's the same gospel. So I guess to your question, for that reason, I'm trying to think when or why I would want to say the gospel of Paul in contradistinction to some other kind of gospel, because it seems to just work into this kind of "Jesus versus Paul," "kingdom versus justification." But maybe there's some helpful way I'm not thinking of.

DAC: What I was after was really two things, and you've mentioned one of them already. That is to say, in the first century—this has been very clearly shown by many people, especially Martin Hengel—what was understood was that it was the gospel of Jesus Christ according to Matthew, the gospel of Jesus Christ according to Mark, the gospel of Jesus Christ according to Luke, and so on.

So they were the witnesses bearing witness to the one true gospel. That's why, for all of us who have taken first-year baby Greek and get our first feel of a New Testament in our hands . . . we open it up and we see the first words on the page of the New Testament—*Kata Matthaion*, "According to Matthew." It's not the gospel *of* Matthew. It's the gospel of Jesus Christ *to* Matthew, and through him to his readers. Eventually, the term *gospel*, late in the second and in the third century, came to refer to a genre of literature. So, Gospels as opposed to Epistles. But in the first century, nobody used the term that way. There was no such things as *a* Gospel in a literary sense. It was *the* gospel of Jesus Christ according to Matthew, Mark, Luke, and John. And it was only later that the term came to be associated with the literary genre. But, then, the second element is: What do you do with an expression like "the gospel of the kingdom"? Is that a subset, an equivalent, an alternative? That is, after all, a biblical category. What does it mean?

JP: To intensify the question, Jesus came preaching the gospel of the kingdom. That's Matthew. And here's Matthew 24:14: "This gospel of the kingdom will be preached throughout all the world as a testimony to all the nations and then the end will come," which means, in Jesus's mind, what he was preaching would be preached to the end. And my take on that is he looked at what Paul did and said: "That's exactly what I mean. You're doing it. You're doing it." He did not mean: "Mimic my phraseology, which is being formulated carefully to get me to the cross at the appointed hour and not an hour sooner by the people who are trying to make me king because I fed their bellies. I need to get to the cross and show you what a king is, what kings are like, in the kingdom, so that you can preach the gospel of the crucified kingdom forever"—which is what Paul and the apostles helped us do.

DAC: You know, you referred earlier when we were having supper to an essay by a young scholar at Cambridge, in which he works out three patterns of understanding the relationship between us and God in the Gospels and in Paul. Do you want to outline that? I thought that that was very helpful.

TK: Well, Simon Gathercole, who's now at Cambridge, wrote an article about the gospel of Paul and the gospel of Jesus—or the supposed gospels of Paul and Jesus. He felt that when Paul talked about the gospel, the three elements in Paul's gospel were: who Jesus is—he's the incarnate son of David; secondly, he died for atonement and justification; and then thirdly, Jesus brings the new creation. I mean, Paul is very eschatological if you read Romans 8, and even what Dick Gaffin always points out with Titus, where Paul's talking about essentially the future renewal of all things is coming into my life now through the new birth. And so, the third thing Paul talks about—after who Jesus is and his death for atonement and justification—and then he brings in the new creation, which is seen, yes, more in terms, in Paul, of how individually we are freed from the dominion of sin. We're freed from the kingdom of sin and brought into the kingdom of his dear Son. So it's a little more to do with freedom from the dominion of sin in the new creation. And then, Gathercole says, you go to the Synoptics, and what you have is Jesus the Messiah, so he's the prophesied Messiah. You have Jesus's death for many. He gave his life a ransom for many. That's a little Pauline bomb in the middle of Mark and Matthew. But then, of course, there's the reign of God over the demons. He would say that in the Synoptics, there's more talk about Jesus overcoming the demonic in the world and delivering us from the demonic. Paul would talk more about deliverance from indwelling sin. But he says those three same elements, which are who is Jesus, death for many, and the new creation and the reign of God, are really all three there. The thing I think we have to make sure before we're done is to talk about in what way the term *kingdom* adds value—the way the Synoptic preaching of Jesus goes. What value does that add? Because I don't believe that it would be in the canon unless God wanted us to say when you preach it like this—here's the John way of eternal life, here's the Synoptics' way of the kingdom of God, here's Paul's way more on justification and the dominion of sin—don't they basically inform each other? Don't they actually give us a fuller and richer understanding of salvation? I think so. But that essay is in a compendium called *God's Power to Save*. That's where Simon Gathercole's article is, and in fact, the whole volume is about that.

DAC: Edited by Chris Green.

TK: Yeah. It's edited by Chris Green. Oak Hill Annual School of Theology. *God's Power to Save.*[2] Really, basically on the subject we're talking about here tonight.

KD: Can I start to answer that? And then I'll let these guys clean it up. Why the kingdom language and what value does it have? Obviously Jesus often speaks that way. I think what you said is exactly right. The kingdom is the heavenly rule and reign. It's eternal life breaking in here. I think of it as the sun that is there and then it breaks through the clouds with greater intensity. It comes into our world in increasing amounts . . . kingdom comes in that way. What is this heavenly world going to be like? There's not going to be any want or scarcity or poverty. Well, that has something to say about the kingdom here and now. What is this kingdom to come, this heavenly realm? Well, everyone bows the knee to Christ. That's why, even now, you have to acknowledge the King, repent and believe in the King, to be a part of the kingdom. There are no wicked in the consummated kingdom. Sometimes people say we have to be working at all these things to affect the kingdom in our world. Yes and no. Before we go too far down that line, we remember that in the kingdom, there are no wicked people; so does that mean that we go and punish all of them and throw them into the lake of fire? Well, no, because the church is a kind of outpost of the kingdom where those heavenly realities and virtues and values come to bear, so that church discipline is a kind of precursor to that kingdom ethic. The church having everything in common so that no one was

---

[2] Chris Green, ed., *God's Power to Save: One Gospel for a Complex World?* (Nottingham, UK: Inter-Varsity Press, 2006).

in want was that heavenly ethic coming down into the context of the church, and, we might say, it's not completely circumscribed by those boundaries. But I think that's where the kingdom becomes incredibly helpful for what it is God is doing right now in establishing his rule and reign. Some of that heavenly reality that we can enjoy is breaking in right now. And I would say that is located in the church. That would be an interesting discussion we could have.

DAC: I'm happy to go down that line, but let me ask a subset question first just to push this a little bit further. A lot of the contemporary discussions speak quite a bit of kingdom ethics, kingdom this, kingdom that—where *kingdom* is essentially an adjective, although in the New Testament, it's just never an adjective at all. It is a noun, or as a verb, "God reigns." Is there any appropriateness to speaking of kingdom ethics and kingdom self-denial and kingdom generosity and kingdom this or that and so on? Or is that usage taking us astray?

KD: I'm talking too much, but I would say if you take that analogy of the kingdom outpost, a sort of an embassy of another world—if you have your country's embassy in another country, you're there to advance the purposes of some foreign nation. And so you live by the rules of the foreign nation. You're there to further its mission. So, in that way, I think you could say we are here as Christians and in the church, an outpost of another kingdom breaking in. And in that sense, we're going to live according to the rules of that kingdom, advance the mission of that kingdom, that we're here in this world, but our allegiance is primarily to another. And in that way, I think you could say there's kingdom ethics.

TK: Yeah, our citizenship is in heaven. I've always found that intriguing, though, because if you're an ambassador—that is, if you're a citizen of another country, but you come to a new country—you're representing the country you came from. You're not just an immigrant, really. And yet, at the same time, you do have to live here and you have to show great respect and you have to know the language. I think that ambassador idea is not only useful in preaching that, but there are many aspects to it. The more you meditate on it, the more it gives you insights as to what it means to be a Christian in the world today. I think, in that sense too, I agree with Kevin, that you can say the idea of kingdom ethics means you come from a place where the values are very different. Michael Wilcock has a great little exposition of Luke, in which he talks about the upside-down values of the kingdom in Luke 6, where Jesus essentially says the things the world loves the kingdom doesn't, and the things the kingdom loves the world doesn't, so he says recognition, power, fame, all the things in the world—that's the coinage of the realm. In the kingdom, those things aren't valuable. In fact, the opposites are valuable—humility is valuable. In all that sense, yes, I would absolutely say that there's a way in which you can talk about the values of my homeland, which I want to represent and live according to in this foreign land—in that sense, yes, we could be talking about kingdom ethics. I think so.

Now, have you heard it used in a way that you don't like, Don or John?

JP: Yes. I don't like the term. If somebody used it, I would just say, "What do you mean?" And then, I would decide whether I agreed or not. But the term to me smacks of a resistance to the flow of the New Testament, because if I were to use the term—which I could do since the kingdom has come, I do live in it, I have a King and I am his ambassador, and I ought to behave in a certain way because of it, and you could call that kingdom ethics. I could use that. Paul never, I don't think, comes close to using it that way. Well, he comes close perhaps in Colossians—we've been transferred out of the kingdom of darkness into the kingdom of his beloved Son, and that has moral implications in Colossians. But what I'd want to know is when you say "kingdom ethics," do you mean you have moved through Jesus's life, his death and resurrection, the outpouring of the Holy Spirit, and you're taking your cue from authoritative apostles who are showing us how to build and nurture the church? If so, do you mean Romans 6? Do you mean Romans 12? Do you mean Ephesians 4–6? Do you mean 1 Peter 2? If they said, "Yes, that's what I mean," I'd say, "Not a problem." But I don't think that's what's usually meant. I don't think so. I think it's used by people who are a little disillusioned with talk about the fruit of the Holy Spirit or about being transformed by the renewing of your mind because of the mercies of God. All that Epistle talk about how you move toward holiness, they don't want to go there. They want to get back fifty years and plant themselves in the Sermon on the Mount or somewhere, and distance themselves. And I go just the opposite. I'm going to stake my life—what's left of it—on the fact that the New Testament and the apostles represent what one ought to make of Jesus for the church. One ought to make Romans. One ought to make 1 Corinthians. One ought to make Colossians and Galatians—that's the way the apostles did Jesus for the church. They didn't go back and try to restate it.

Interesting appeal to Don here—I remember when I was work-ing on my degree, the Scandinavians had this sense that the tradi-tion, the oral tradition, being preserved of the sayings and acts of Jesus was running parallel with the application of it in epistolary language, because they would say there's almost no doubt that early Christians were told the sorts of things Jesus did and said, and all the scholars are scratching their heads: "Why isn't it showing up more in the Epistles?" And the answer was that this was almost like a sacred tradition, had Jewish counterparts, and here's the way it got applied. And that's what's preserved for us. So whether that's accurate or not as a possible explanation, what we do know is that we have Paul and Peter and James, and they are authoritative for us for how to nurture and care for the church. But I totally agree with where you were going in saying, "But don't all the pieces make sig-nificant contributions?" And I would say absolutely they do, and if you ask, then, Paul or the person trying to read Romans 12 or 6 in terms of ethics, if there is any emphasis that could be brought to that from the kingdom emphasis of the Epistles, the answer would be yes. There would be great light to be shown. He's King, and look at what he did with the kingdom.

TK: Right. Even when Paul's talking about, in Romans 14, being very practical about dealing with the various factions in the church, being merciful to each other, and honoring each other's consciences, and all that, he asserts that the kingdom of God is not a matter of eating or drinking, but of righteousness, joy, and peace in the Holy Spirit. That is very clearly an ethical thrust. But he's not just saying exactly that here are ethical principles of behavior. He's trying to say something about the fact that in the kingdom of God we shouldn't behave like this. So there's an ethical thrust, and yet it's not just a set of ethics.

JP: I would say you're absolutely right about what that very sentence does, "The kingdom of God is not eating or drinking, but righteousness, peace, joy *in the Holy Spirit.*" Paul would say I'm showing you how to talk about the kingdom now.

TK: Well, that's what's so intriguing, because he really does equate life in the Spirit with the kingdom of God. And he has no problem with that. He's not pitting them against each other.

KD: So if I hear you, John, your concern with just making *kingdom* an adjective is that folks who are eager to get to what they see as the ethics of Jesus don't think they have to go through doctrine and they don't have to go through any of these other categories. And that's what you see sometimes in a sophisticated way and sometimes in a clumsy way: "Isn't this wonderful, we've got Jesus and we've got kingdom." . . . Like an evangelist at Michigan State one time ended with a climax of holding up a red crayon and saying, "Who wants to go paint the world red for Jesus?" It was kind of "Make a difference and follow in Jesus's footsteps"—and, of course, it left out the biggest footstep, which is the cross. And you've said many times, we have to read the Gospels backward. I mean, I got that from you—Matthew 1:21.

JP: Right. "Read the Gospels backward" means, in order for me to grasp what Luke is trying to do in chapters 1 and 2, I really do need to know how the forgiveness of sins is going to be worked out, and Luke certainly did not intend for me to read chapters 1 and 2, close the book, and go try to live that way. He wanted the whole book to have its whole message, and then, I would add, the whole New Testament—and, in fact, all sixty-six books.

KD: Amen. Amen.

JP: So I really dislike "canon within a canon" talk or "start here and it makes all the difference" talk. I want us to be a people who take it all seriously and ask a question at any given point we're interpreting a piece of Paul or a piece of Jesus: Is there anything in Paul that would make this interpretation of Jesus look wrong? If that's true, I've probably gotten it wrong. Is there anything that I'm interpreting over here in Paul that anything over here from Jesus would make that look wrong? If so, I've probably got this wrong. And so I'm constantly being helped and corrected and refined in my theology by taking all of it seriously wherever I start.

DAC: Let me complexify the subject one more notch, if I may. In a handful of cases in the Old Testament, specifically, but then everywhere in the Bible thematically, God is presented as the great King over all. He does what he wills in the armies of heaven. He does what he wills among men. Not a bird falls from the heavens, according to Jesus, apart from his sanction. In Proverbs, you throw the dice and which numbers come up, that's under God's sovereignty. And so, God's kingdom rules over all, and in that sense, we're all in the kingdom, whether we like it or not. You can be an atheist, a Buddhist, a Muslim, you can be a secularist—it doesn't matter where you are or where you were born, you're in the kingdom. Now, some uses of kingdom language in the Gospels are that embracing and some are not. So when Jesus, for example, in a parable likens the kingdom to wheat and tares, it includes both wheat and tares. That is, in the sweep of God's sovereignty, one finds both wheat and tares. Similarly, after the resurrection, Jesus says, "All authority is given to me in heaven and on earth." And yet, there are lots of other kingdom references in which, at the risk of using mechanical or spatial language, the kingdom is that subset of God's total kingdom under which there is life, some subset of the totality of God's sovereignty under which there is eternal life. And that subset is coming, and yet, at the same time, while that subset is coming, you are either in it or you're not. Yet, in some sense, you are under Christ's authority now. Christ's reign is all of God's sovereignty mediated through him until the last enemy is destroyed, namely, death itself, and then, God is made all in all. And that is another element of kingdom that is sometimes left out of this discussion. In other words, *kingdom* is used in rather diverse ways. So let me hear how you guys are going to integrate such phenomena into everything that we have said.

JP: You said right, so we must agree.

TK: I'm all for it! I think it's interesting that Jesus says to Pilate, "My kingdom is not of this world." So right there he's using it differently than the providential kingdom, and yet, almost in the same breath, he says to Pilate, "You've got no power except that which my Father gave you." In other words, "The only reason that you've got power to crucify me is you're actually doing my Father's will right now." It's intriguing that he almost talks about the two aspects—in one sense, "My kingdom is not here, it's not of this world." Meaning, it's not a political kingdom. It's a spiritual kingdom of people who are born again. And yet, he almost turns right around and says, "And yet you're only doing what the great King of history and the universe wants you to do." Not that he uses the word *kingdom* twice, but very much—they're both there in that very same passage—those two aspects. It's very *complexifying*.

KD: Yeah. It seems like it's some of that "already" and "not yet"— just like there are different ways in which the term *world* can be used. So God is the King over all things and Christ is the King right now, whether anyone in this room acknowledges it or not, whether we sing another song, whether anyone in this whole country . . . he is King. We don't make him King. He is. And yet, when he comes back, every knee will bow and every tongue confess that he is Lord to the glory of God the Father. It seems like one of the closest passages to what you are talking about, Don, is Hebrews 2: "Now in putting everything in subjection to him, he left nothing outside his control. [That seems somewhat absolute already.] At present we do not yet see everything in subjection to him. But we see him who for a little while was made lower than the angels, namely Jesus, crowned with glory and honor, because of the suffering of death." So he is a King, has been a King, is a coming King, and bringing more people into his kingdom.

DAC: And sometimes under that usage of King, there is a subset in which you are either in it or not. And that needs to be integrated with this broader sense in which he is ruling, but his rule is still contested until one day there is no contestation. But there is still this subset usage that, unless you're born again, you cannot see, you cannot enter the kingdom of God. That means some are in and some are not. It's not just the question of it having dawned and he is reigning, but it's being contested, there's some usage of *kingdom* in which the locus is not as broad as the complete sovereignty of God mediated through Christ. And it's important to get those things clear, it seems to me, as we are teaching Scripture.

TK: Here's another aspect of kingdom, in a sense, because to-morrow in the afterconference—*plug*—we'll be talking about the integration of faith and work. Now, this gets us into an area that Abraham Kuyper talked about. By the way, he's Dutch. You would've liked him. Kuyper, of course, said that because Jesus is Lord, that means he is not only Lord over your private life, but every area of your life. Simple. And I think, increasingly in this country, as you might say, as the public culture becomes colder to Christians, it will get easier and easier for us to seal our public life and our work life off from our faith. That is to say, my faith is for giving me personal peace and help in my private life, but when it comes to thinking about how it affects the way in which I do business and the way I do politics, how it's worked out in the world, I don't want to go there because it's complex and I haven't figured it out. But Abraham Kuyper, by lifting up the kingship of Christ over every area of life, forces you into whole-life disciple-ship. He forces you to see that it's not just my Savior that gives me eternal life so I'll live forever. He's the King, and every area of my life is under his kingship. I have to ask: "Am I really doing his will as a banker? I'm a banker. Am I just being conformed to this world?" I mean, what does the Bible say about how I should be living my life under Christ that has an implication on how I do banking? And you have to ask that question. And I think there's another way in which the kingdom is of value—if you don't have that word in there, especially Americans: we don't like the idea of having a king. We want someone who meets our needs. We don't want someone who rules over us. And that's another aspect where the kingdom language adds value.

DAC: Many of the categories of Scripture do not resonate with anything in the culture. And kingdom is one of them. The United States is a republic. The kingdom we think most of, if we are think-ing of any, is the British monarchy, which is constitutional, and God is not a constitutional monarch. And then priest—how many of us go through our lives thinking whether or not we have an ade-quate priest? Covenant. We don't use that terminology in everyday speech. So many of the categories of Scripture are not categories that are current in everyday life, but they have to become pas-sionately current in our understanding and thinking in the church and in our lives or we simply won't understand Scripture. But al-though Kuyper's emphasis on—you know, "Not one square foot is there any place in the universe where Jesus does not say, 'This is mine!'"—yet, there's a flip side danger to that. You can be so busy talking about how this is God's all over—that you are thinking about God's complete sovereignty, and we're under God's sovereignty, and thinking of the way these things work out in various spheres—that we forget that there is this subset use of kingdom language where you are either in or out. If you start thinking of God's sovereignty with only respect to everything, which is a huge theme—I'm not trying to depreciate it at all—but overlook that there is a subset in which people are either in or out, you're either in that kingdom or you're not, then it seems to me that it's easy to start thinking strategically at the global and political and working level and forget, at the same time, you still have to preach, "You must be born again."

KD: And to complexify that, Reformed theologians have often distinguished between the different ways in which Christ reigns over all things. So there's that general sovereignty, and there's that mediatorial reign where he reigns by his Word in the church. And so, amen, and yes, amen, everyone should say to Abraham Kuyper's favorite phrase, and yet, you need to nuance it, or otherwise it becomes just a mess of, well, Christ ought to reign over everything or he's exercising that reign now in exactly the same way.

TK: Yeah, in other words, a utopianism or triumphalism—so that's why we've got to have Don around to complexify otherwise—well, actually, what is so rich about the kingdom of God is—we've even talked about the "already" but "not yet"—but Don likes to give you about five things. It's not just "already" but "not yet," but it's *completely* here in terms of providential rule. It's not here in terms of—there's so many ways in which you can talk about it. Where have you written that down? I know I've read it three or four times. Where would be the closest, fastest way for people to get your work on the kingdom?

DAC: Don't have a clue. I mean, I wrote somewhere probably two or three times, but I don't have a clue. Sorry!

TK: See, we have the same problem now. I know I wrote it somewhere. So—but hey, listen. Can I end on a negative note?

DAC: Pardon?

TK: I'd like to end on a negative note.

KD: Tim Keller?

DAC: Well, you can give us the negative note and then we'll decide if that will end it.

TK: Well, not really. I would like to go back to where we were going, and that is, I am very unhappy with people trying to take the kingdom—and I've seen a number of younger ministers over the last ten to fifteen years get this way—and to say that's the gospel—"Jesus is Lord." That's the gospel—"The kingdom of God is at hand." Initially it seems more biblical. It seems more Jesus. And so, I have seen people say here's the gospel presentation—the gospel presentation is that Jesus Christ came here and established his kingdom. It's not completely here, but it's really a people of God, a people now who are carrying out his kingdom program to renew the world and to work for peace and justice, and you need to join it. And that's what ends up happening. And I have to say— you know, you've probably heard me say it, perhaps, before—I said, if that's the gospel, where or why would you ever sing, "My chains fell off, my heart was free, I rose went forth and followed thee"? Where's the release? Where's the joy? Where's the transformation? It just sounds like you're joining another program. And it's a kind of a liberal works righteousness . . . just taking the word *kingdom* to mean living a great life and making the world a great place and working for peace and justice and putting that in as your gospel presentation. If that's what you're calling people to do, it's, I think, very damaging and it's not good. And, I think, in some ways behind everything else we've said here tonight is that: the tendency on the part of a lot of young ministers in the last ten to fifteen years to get romantic about the term *kingdom* and just begin to use it everywhere and not really see all the complexities of it.

DAC: Richard Baxter, when he was arguing about justification—whether one likes everything he says about justification or not—one of the wise things that he says is if someone comes into your town preaching an erroneous view of justification, don't begin by refuting him. Preach up—that's his expression—preach up justification better than he. And in exactly the same way, if we see the notion of kingdom being abused in various forms of reductionism, then our first response must be to preach up the kingdom better than they. That is to get it right biblically again and again and again and again. And within that framework, to show how the reductionisms do not square with Scripture and ultimately do damage to Christ and to the gospel and to the church for which Christ shed his blood. Rather than, simply, sounding censorious and consigning people to the bottom level of Dante's Inferno.

Would you like to close us in prayer, please?

KD: Our gracious heavenly Father, what a privilege that we can come to you as your adopted children and call you our Father. And we praise you because of the work of your Holy Spirit through the Word in our lives. We praise you because of your Son, our Lord Jesus Christ, the resurrected once and coming King. And we pray in his name, knowing that he who began a good work in us will be faithful to complete it. And knowing that one day when he returns, the kingdom of this world will become, for all time, the kingdom of our Lord and of His Christ. And we pray that you would hasten that day and if you were to give us any small part in being ambassadors for that great and glorious good news, we would be most privileged. We pray that you would fill us with your Spirit, that you would guard the truth, that you would help us to be men and women of all the Book—of the whole counsel of God, using the terms, the vocabulary, the nuances, never pitting one against another. O Lord, we thank you for this Book that you have given to us and for the Spirit who inspired all of it and now gives us the gift of illumination that we might understand it, interpret it, apply it, and, amazingly enough, even begin to live it out. Be with us now in the remainder of our evening and may all we think and do and say be fitting for those who worship Jesus as King. In his name, Amen.

CONTRIBUTORS

D. A. Carson

D. A. Carson (PhD, University of Cambridge) is cofounder and president of The Gospel Coalition and since 1978 has taught at Trinity Evangelical Divinity School (Deerfield, IL), where he currently serves as Research Professor of New Testament. He came to Trinity from Northwest Baptist Theological Seminary in Vancouver, British Columbia, and has served in pastoral ministry in Canada and the United Kingdom. He and his wife, Joy, have two children.

Kevin DeYoung

Kevin DeYoung (MDiv, Gordon-Conwell Theological Seminary) has been the senior pastor at University Reformed Church in East Lansing, Michigan, since August 2004. Prior to serving at URC, Kevin was the associate pastor at First Reformed Church in Orange City, Iowa. Kevin and his wife, Trisha, have six children.

Tim Keller

Tim Keller serves as senior pastor of Redeemer Presbyterian Church in Manhattan, a church he planted in 1989, with his wife, Kathy, and their three sons. Originally from Pennsylvania, he was educated at Bucknell University; Gordon-Conwell Theological Seminary; and Westminster Theological Seminary. He is cofounder and vice president of The Gospel Coalition.

Crawford Loritts

Crawford Loritts (DD, Biola University) is the senior pastor of Fellowship Bible Church in Roswell, Georgia, where he lives with his wife, Karen. In 1978, he joined the staff of Campus Crusade for Christ (Cru), and now serves as associate director for Cru-USA, helping shape Cru's national ministry, mentoring younger leaders, and representing the organization through his speaking and writing ministry.

Gary Millar

Gary Millar (DPhil, University of Oxford) is principal of Queensland Theological College in Brisbane, Australia. A Northern Irishman, Gary is married to Fiona, a Scot born in Peru of missionary parents, and they have three daughters. Before moving to Brisbane at the beginning of 2012, the Millars spent 12 years in Dublin, Ireland, where Gary pastored a pair of Presbyterian churches, as well as teaching at the Irish Bible Institute.

John Piper

John Piper is founder and teacher of Desiring God (DesiringGod.org), chancellor of Bethlehem College and Seminary, and a founding council member of The Gospel Coalition. For thirty-three years he served as senior pastor at Bethlehem Baptist Church (Minneapolis). He studied at Wheaton College; Fuller Theological Seminary (BD); and the University of Munich (DTh). He and his wife, Noel, have four sons, one daughter, and a growing number of grandchildren.

Colin Smith

Colin Smith (MPhil, London School of Theology) is senior pastor of The Orchard Evangelical Free Church in Arlington Heights (IL), and his ministry extends through his radio program *Unlocking the Bible*. He is also committed to mentoring next-generation pastors through The Orchard Network. Colin and his wife, Karen, have two sons and two granddaughters.

Stephen Um

Stephen Um (PhD, University of St. Andrews) is senior pastor of Citylife Presbyterian Church of Boston. He also teaches New Testament at Gordon-Conwell Theological Seminary, and serves as Associate Training Director with Redeemer City to City. Stephen and his wife, Kathleen, have been involved in several Presbyterian churches throughout the northeastern United States.

GENERAL INDEX

SCRIPTURE INDEX

THE GOSPEL **COALITION**

The Gospel Coalition is a fellowship of evangelical churches deeply committed to renewing our faith in the gospel of Christ and to reforming our ministry practices to conform fully to the Scriptures. We have committed ourselves to invigorating churches with new hope and compelling joy based on the promises received by grace alone through faith alone in Christ alone.

We desire to champion the gospel with clarity, compassion, courage, and joy—gladly linking hearts with fellow believers across denominational, ethnic, and class lines. We yearn to work with all who, in addition to embracing our confession and theological vision for ministry, seek the lordship of Christ over the whole of life with unabashed hope in the power of the Holy Spirit to transform individuals, communities, and cultures.

Join the cause and visit TGC.org for fresh resources that will equip you to love God with all your heart, soul, mind, and strength, and to love your neighbor as yourself.

TGC.org